Places To Be

A compendium of
transformational holidays
and places to "just be"

CW01551760

Includes venues in Barbados,
France, Germany, Greece, India,
Ireland, Italy, Portugal, Spain,
Sri Lanka and Turkey.
Plus a selection of Alternative
Holiday and Tour Operators!

2005

Edited by Jonathan How and William Morris

Places to BE 2005
© Coherent Visions 2004
ISBN: 0 9524396 7 0

Editing and Design
Jonathan How and William Morris

Publisher
Coherent Visions, BCM Visions
London WC1N 3XX
℡ 0870 444 2566
✆ info@places-to-be.com

Printer
Buckingham Colour Press
1 Osier Way, Swan Business Pk
Buckingham MK18 1TB
℡ 01280 824 000
✆ info@buckinghamcolour.
com

Distributor
Edge of Time Ltd
BCM Edge, London
WC1N 3XX
℡ 0800 083 0451

While the editors have made every effort to ensure that the information we include in this book is accurate and up to date, we would encourage you to be aware that things may change, particularly some years after publication, and to be sensitive around this when contacting organisations in this book. Furthermore, we accept information in good faith, and while we know and love many of the organisations herein, we are not endorsing them, and you must take responsibility for ensuring that they meet your needs. We're always happy to receive positive and constructive feedback.

Contents

PLACES-TO-BE
.COM

Introduction

You hold in your hands the latest edition of a book that, for ten years now, has guided people to new places and new experiences.

With its Seekers' Indexes, Places to Be was the first publication in Britain to present information about centres in an ordered way. Ten years and eight editions on, the book now includes many overseas holistic holiday venues and operators as well as dozens of more local "B&Bs with a difference". It is the definitive guide.

You may be looking for a healing retreat, a walking holiday, or a venue where you can run your own courses. You will find this and much more in Places to Be.

The experiences available from the organisations in this book are many and varied, but above all you will probably grow in your understanding of your own path in life. You are likely to find other friendly, interesting people, and you may be able to inspire and encourage each other along the way. Even now, a few years into the new century, we are still encouraged to fit in with certain images of who we're meant to be, what we're meant to believe, and how we're meant to interact with each other, on personal and economic levels. Our frenetic lifestyles often key us ever more firmly into the materialist visions of global business.

Many of the people who are offering tours, workshops, retreats and other places to stay have broken free of the mould, and are creating a new, gentler and more sustainable reality. You can be part of this, and add your own energy, vision and creativity.

Many of the places and holiday operators in this book are inspired by spiritual and/or political beliefs, and many are aware of the need to create a sustainable, Earth-friendly way of being. You have the chance to travel to beautiful and unusual places in the world and experience living in harmony with the landscape and culture. Look out for the eco-tourism features which many venues and organisations describe.

Several of the venues in this book are set in intentional communities of people living co-operatively. Age after age these places have been on the forward edge of social change, and if you are interested in this way of life, or of making links to it, then the events that they run provide a wonderful opportunity.

All of the venues and holidays in Places to Be are special in some way, offering something that you won't often find. In these pages we have tried to indicate which venues and holidays offer only vegetarian food, which have disabled access and which are particularly welcoming to lesbians and gay men.

You can use the indexes to find, amongst other things, which places welcome children, and which have child-minding facilities. So you as parents can go to workshops, or just be on your own for a while. If you are looking for a venue for a group you are organising, you will find that a lot of the relevant hiring information is now concentrated in one place on a venue's page.

As editors of this book, we allow venue and holiday operators to write at length about themselves, so you get a real flavour of how they are. Many also have websites, where you can read more, and often see helpful pictures.

Our own website, www.places-to-be.com, offers useful search facilities, and is updated during the year so you can be as sure as possible of having current information. In many cases, you will find colour photographs, as well as links to detailed location maps and the organisations' own web sites.

You will find that the book is divided into regions within the UK and countries outside the UK. In addition there is the popular section devoted to holiday and tour operators. As well as the full page entries which many venues desire, there are additional listings of other known venues. These are places whose existence we are fairly sure of (eg they have current websites) but for one reason or another they haven't replied to our requests for information.

Never just turn up at any of the places listed in this book. Always make arrangements beforehand and in this way you will be sure of a welcome. The essential prerequisite of a positive retreat experience.

Let this 10th Anniversary Edition be your way into a host of new holiday and holiday possibilities!

If you enjoy this book then you may be interested in other products distributed by Edge of Time. Phone for a catalogue on 0800 083 0451 or visit **www.edgeoftime.co.uk**.

Diggers & Dreamers

This directory is known as the communard's bible and its new small format is proving very popular. It gives you an up-to-date directory of more than 80 existing and embryonic communities within the UK. Everything from Anarres to Zion! The 2004/05 edition also features: a useful cross-index to help you find the community that matches your preferences; icons indicating how each community operates; 10 myths of communal living exploded; a listing of Networks and Support Organisations

Thinking about CoHousing

CoHousing projects are all about building neighbour-hoods as if people mattered. Over the past 30 years they have spread from Denmark to the USA, but only recently have they appeared in the UK. This book is not a complete handbook but a look at what CoHousing is and what it isn't. It outlines strategies for creating CoHousing neigh-bourhoods and features case studies as well as sections on: designing CoHousing neigh-bourhoods; legal structures; finance; and training.

Moonwise Calendar

In this lunar calendar the months begin with New Moon, moon phases are shown for each night, and there are festi-vals and secular holidays from all round the world. All this plus fabulous illustrations. The Moonwise Calendar is of particular interest to Pagans, useful for people of many tra-ditions, and full of information and inspiration. An unusual and fascinating gift for your friends, family and self!

Moonwise Diary

This companion to the Moonwise Calendar is easy to use, with four pages for each week. It contains daily astro-logical information and moon phases; clock times for Britain and Ireland; rising and setting of sun and moon for London, Glasgow and Dublin; as well as outstanding artwork and writ-ing contributed by readers. Small enough to go in your bag or pocket, this diary allows you to work closely with the cycles of the moon, the planets and the peoples of the Earth.

Neal's Yard Agency

The Travel Agent for Inner Journeys

**If you are seeking,
then you will find . . .
at
'The Travel Agent
for Inner Journeys'**

**The UK's leading source of information
for Yoga, creativity & wellbeing holidays**

meditation, massage, creative writing, singing,
dancing, simply 'being', unspoilt locations, yurts,
tree houses, hammocks, like-minded company,
laughter, fun, discovery ...

For free Holiday & Events Guide
contact
Neal's Yard Agency
BCM Neal's Yard • London WC1N 3XX • UK
Tel 0870 444 2702 • info@nealsyardagency.com
www.nealsyardagency.com

Getting started

The bulk of the book is made up of national and regional sections containing the detailed description of fixed venues. If you're just idly browsing then this is the place to do it!

The maps are also very useful overviews of what is available in Scotland, Wales and the English regions. **Look out especially for the places shown in bold, as these have full page entries.**

Retreats

People have been going on retreats for hundreds, if not thousands, of years. This ancient form of getting away from it all is rising in popularity again, notably amongst people who do not see themselves as attached to a particular religion. Many Christian establishments cater for this demand, often on a large scale. There are also a growing number of smaller venues offering retreats. You need to check whether the retreats are for individuals or groups; whether they are based on any particular spiritual system; how much guidance is available and/or how much you will be left to your own devices.

Retreat Seeker's Index
page 142

B&Bs

The B&Bs listed in Places to Be are all different in some way, even if that way is simply that they offer vegetarian food (however, this book does not claim to contain a comprehensive listing of vegetarian B&Bs to which several good guides exist already). Many of those in Places to Be are representative of a new breed of B&B which offer something more than just food and accommodation. Perhaps it is some kind of educational service, perhaps a healing therapy.

B&B Seeker's Index
page 139

Holiday and Tour Operators

The organisations listed on pages 131-138 run either touring holidays or else events at a number of venues – some within and some outside the United Kingdom.

Workshops

If you're keen to participate in workshops and courses then head for the **Workshop Seeker's Index**. Here venues are shown with subject speciality headings. Of course, these categories can only be a very crude guide; a place offering walking, for example, will be included within the "Outdoor activities and sport" category. Often the text on the venue's page is more specific, but do look at their websites and/or contact them for more detailed information.

Workshop Seeker's Index
page 146

Map of Scotland: page 10

Details of subject specialities: page 146

Feature on our website: page 152

Venues

If you run courses or workshops yourself then you'll be wanting the Venue Seeker's Index. You'll probably find it easiest to start with the approximate numbers of bedspaces. Where possible the index shows prices, a level of wheelchair access and a number of other accommodation features. You can usually find more specifics in the full pages entries. Always contact the venue for more details and to check that the information has not changed.

Venue Seeker's Index
page 157

Full Page Entries

Venues are arranged alphabetically within nation and region. The text is written by the people who run the venues and tours, and give a good flavour of each. We have also asked them to bring out for you various areas such as spiritual focus, eco-tourism features and public transport access.

Many organisations list broad areas of Subject specialities. See the **Workshop Seeker's Index** for more on these. Suitability and Specialism indicates courses and holidays aimed at or premises suited to particular groups.

Scotland

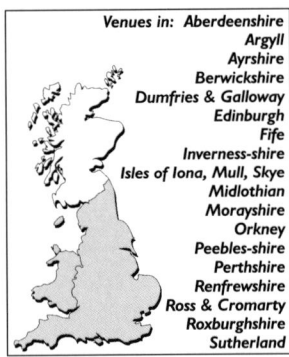

Woodwick
◇ Orkney Images

3 Castle Terrace
Avalon ◇ Choraidh Croft
Suilven

Shanti Griha 14 ◆
Quiraing Lodge ◇ ◇ Corry Lodge ◇ Fearn
Aultguish ◇ ◇ Rhanich
Foxwood ◇

NewBold House 13
Findhaven
Neptune Light House

Findhorn 12 ◆
◆ ◇ Pluscarden Abbey

Centre of Light ◇
◇ Lazy Duck
Avingormack ◇ ◇ Dryburn
Rhu Mhor ◇ Sonnhalde ◇ ◇ Jenny's Bothy
Glengorm ◇ ◇ Cuildorag Inverdeen

Bishop's House ◇◇
St Columba ◇ Glengarry ◇ ◇ Tigh a Gharraidh
Isle of Erraid

◇ St Mary's
Tabor Trust ◇
Cruachan ◇ Blackruthven ◇ **◆ Burgh Lodge 11**

Castle Rock
Greenhouse
Number One
Salisbury Centre

GLASGOW ■
EDINBURGH
East Lochhead ◇ ◇ Carberry
◇ Wheatears
Grey Gables ◇ ◇ Dod Mill
Old Sawmill ◇

Beshara ◇ Whitchester
◇ Samye Ling
Penninghame ◇ ◇ Laurieston
◇ Rossan

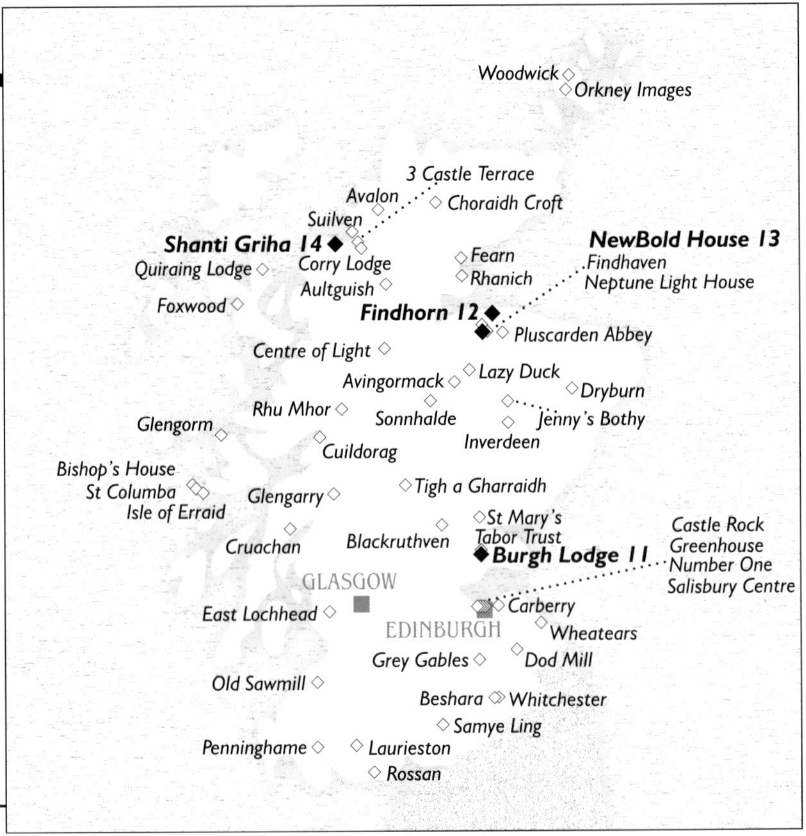

The Burgh Lodge

The Burgh Lodge offers 4 Star value-for-money hostel-style accommodation with a relaxed and friendly atmosphere where guests always receive the warmest of welcomes. Guests can enjoy reading in front of our log fire or explore the medieval and picturesque village of Falkland. A sense of tranquillity and timelessness remains throughout making it an ideal rural getaway for those tired of the City, yet it is within easy reach of Edinburgh, Perth, Stirling, Dundee and St Andrews. The Lodge is surrounded by magnificent walks steeped in mystical scenery and history from times when Mary Queen of Scots and the Royal Stuarts used Falkland for retreats. The Lodge is also within walking distance of our local organic shop and café, making us an ideal destination for those interested in healthy living. The Burgh Lodge is guaranteed to leave you feeling rejuvenated and ready to face everyday life.
£11 pp first night £10pp thereafter, family and larger group discounts; favourable rates for booking entire lodge. Individual self catering, Additional indoor space for larger group meetings is available close by.

Suitability or Specialism
Welcomes Everyone!

Alison Bell
Burgh Lodge, Back Wynd
Falkland, Cupar, Fife
KY15 7BX
✆01337 857710
☏01337 858861
⌨burgh.lodge@btconnect.com

✔ **Bed & Breakfast**
✔ **Venue for hire**
group full board, large indoor space
↘37 bedspaces (2 twins, 2 family, 2 x 4-bed, one 8-bed dormitory). £11/person first night, £10/person thereafter.
♿2 ground floor rooms have specially adapted shower and toilet facilities, fully accessible for guests with disabilities.
🚆Nearest railway station Ladybank 4 miles, or bus to Glenrothes then change to 36 or 66.

Findhorn Foundation

The Park
Findhorn
Forres
Morayshire
IV36 3TZ

© 01309 691620
✆ 01309 691663
✆

communications@findhorn.org

✔ Own Course Programme

⊐ 130 bedspaces.
⦿ Exclusively vegetarian.
✈ Flights are available to
Inverness or Aberdeen then
train or bus to Forres then
taxi to Cluny or The Park.

Focus Non denominational

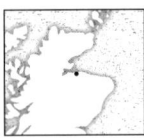

The Findhorn Foundation is the educational and organisational cornerstone of the Findhorn Community, founded in 1962. We are an international centre of spiritual education and personal transformation and a daring experiment in how to live sustainably and in harmony with all of life. Life is rich and challenging as we seek to expand human consciousness through planetary service, cocreation with nature and acknowledging the divinity within all beings. We have two campuses, Cluny Hill College and The Park, and a retreat centre on the island of Iona. We welcome 14,000 visitors a year to tours, workshops and conferences and continue to develop our ecovillage at The Park as a positive and practical way to live sustainably on the earth.

The Findhorn Foundation is an NGO of the United Nations and the Ecovillage Project has been awarded "Best Practice" designation by the United Nations Centre for Human Settlements.

Event Types
Guided group retreats, own course programme, accredited courses.

Subject Specialities
Alternative lifestyles & technology, meditation, food & gardening, health & healing, self expression, arts & crafts, inner process, group process, conservation work, prayer.

Suitability or Specialism
Adults, lesbian women, gay men, young people 12 to 17, older people.

Eco-tourism features
Founding member of the Global Ecovillage Network, organic gardening, windmill, biological sewage treatment plant, recycling, high specification ecohouses, reforestation. Winner of the Green Tourism Business Scheme Gold Award.

NewBold House

NewBold House is a working spiritual community which welcomes guests to join in community life and educational workshops. It offers an integrated experience of living and relating in a different way. The atmosphere created in this beautiful old mansion house and its seven acres of woodland and gardens provides a caring and nurturing environment for individual self-exploration and growth.

Event Types
Self directed retreats.

Suitability or Specialism
Adults.

Newbold House
St Leonards Road
Forres
Morayshire
IV36 2RE

℡ 01309 672659
✉ newbold@findhorn.org

✔ **Retreat House**
✔ **Own Course Programme**

⤳ 30 bedspaces (1 single.)
🍴 Exclusively vegetarian.

Focus New Age

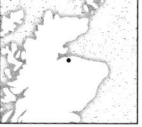

Shanti Griha

Brian & Kathrin Cooper
Shanti Griha
Scoraig Peninsula
Dundonnell, Garve
Wester Ross
IV23 2RE
✆ 01854 633260
✉ shantigriha@hotmail.com

✔ **Retreat House**
✔ **Own Course Programme**
✔ **Venue for hire**
group full board (£35), large indoor space
⌕ 10 bedspaces (4 single, 1 double, 1 family room.)
🍽 Exclusively vegetarian, special diets.
♿ None.
🚌 Bus to Ullapool or Dundonnell, pick up by arrangement.

Focus
Buddhist, Eco-spiritual, Yogic.

Shanti Griha, meaning House of Peace, is a stunning Highland retreat and course centre set in two acres of magical garden on secluded and car-free Scoraig Peninsula in Northwest Scotland. Access is along a three-mile footpath meandering above the rugged coast, where otters, red deer, eagles and wild goats may be spotted. The house has a beautiful bright yoga studio/ meditation room, library and log fire. It is situated at the foot of Ben Ghobhlach and looks out onto Little Loch Broom and the open sea towards the Summer Isles and the

Outer Hebrides. Courses include Yoga, Yoga Teacher Training, Meditation and Buddhism, Traditional Thai Massage, Tai Ji and Qi Gong, Windpower, Dry Stone Walling, Vegetarian Cooking, and Astrology. Courses take place between April and October and are limited to eight participants. Please ask for our brochure. Individual retreats are best booked at short notice and can also be arranged alongside courses. The minimum stay is four nights at £35 per night, which includes all meals, bedding, towels, the use of all our facili-

ties, and Meditation guidance. Thai Massage sessions and Yoga lessons can be booked with Brian and Tai Ji/Qi Gong lessons with Kathrin. Scoraig is dotted with windmills providing electricity to 30 households and it has its own school. Residents include a boatbuilder, violinmaker, pony breeder, potter, weaver, and many wonderfully eccentric folk. There are no shops or restaurants.

Subject Specialities
Yoga, Buddhism, Meditation, Alternative lifestyles & technology. Particularly suitable for Adults. Children by arrangement.

Eco-tourism features
Own windmill, own spring, locally sourced organic food, own organic vegetable garden, herb garden and orchard, home-baked bread.

Other Places and Organisations

3 Castle Terrace B&B
Ullapool
Ross and Cromarty
IV26 2XD
Bed & Breakfast

The Aultguish Inn
Garve
Ross and Cromarty
IV23 2PQ
Bed & Breakfast

Avalon
Elphin, Lairg
Sutherland
IV27 4HH
Bed & Breakfast

Avingormack Guesthouse
Boat of Garten
Inverness-shire
PH24 3BT
Retreat House

Beshara School
Chisholme House
Roberton, Hawick
Roxburghshire
TD9 7PH
Own Course Programme

The Bield at Blackruthven
Tibbermore
Perth
PH1 1PY
Retreat House

Bishop's House
Isle of Iona
Argyll
PA76 6SJ
Retreat House

Carberry
Musselburgh
Midlothian
EH21 8PY
Venue for hire

Castle Rock Hostel
15 Johnston Terrace
Edinburgh
EH1 2PW
Bed & Breakfast

Centre of Light
Tighnabruaich
Struy
Beauly
Inverness-shire
IV4 7JU
Retreat House

Choraidh Croft Farm
94 Laid
Loch Enbollside
Altnaharra
Lairg
Sutherland
IV27 4UN
Bed & Breakfast

Corry Lodge B&B
Garve Road
Lochbroom
Ullapool
Ross and Cromarty
IV26 2TB
Bed & Breakfast

Cruachan
Inverae Farm Road
Minard
Inveraray
Argyll
PA32 8YF
Bed & Breakfast

Other Places and Organisations

Cuildorag House
Onich, Fort William
Inverness-shire
PH33 6SD
Bed & Breakfast

Dod Mill Retreat Centre
Dod Mill House
Lauder, Berwickshire
TD2 6SE
Venue for hire

Dryburn House
Ordhead, Inverurie
Aberdeenshire
AB51 7RL
Bed & Breakfast

East Lochhead
Largs Road, Lochwinnoch
Renfrewshire
PA12 4DX
Bed & Breakfast

Isle of Erraid
Fionnphort
Isle of Mull
Argyll
PA66 6BN
Own Course Programme

Fearn House
High Street
Dornoch
Sutherland
IV25 3SH
Bed & Breakfast

Findhaven
16 Market Street
Forres
Morayshire
IV36 1EF
Bed & Breakfast

Foxwood
11a Ullinish
by Struan
Isle of Skye
IV56 8FD
© 01470 572331
Bed & Breakfast

Glengarry House
Tyndrum
Crianlarich
Perthshire
FK20 8RY
Bed & Breakfast

Glengorm Castle
Tobermory
Isle of Mull
PA75 6QE
Bed & Breakfast

The Greenhouse
14 Hartington Gardens
Bruntsfield
Edinburgh
EH10 4LD
Bed & Breakfast

Grey Gables
Springwood Road
Peebles
EH45 9HB
Bed & Breakfast

Other Places and Organisations

Inverdeen House
11 Bridge Square
Ballater
Aberdeenshire
AB35 5QJ
Bed & Breakfast

Jenny's Bothy
Dellachuper
Corgarff
Strathdon
Aberdeenshire
AB36 8YP
Venue for hire

Laurieston Hall
Laurieston
Castle Douglas
Dumfries and Galloway
DG7 2NB
Own Course Programme

Lazy Duck Bunkhouse
Badanfhuarain, Nethy Bridge
Inverness-shire PH25 3ED
✆ 01479 821643
Venue for hire

Neptune Light House
22-24 Tolbooth Street
Forres, Morayshire
IV36 1PH
Bed & Breakfast

Number One
1 Gayfield Place
Edinburgh
EH7 4AB
Bed & Breakfast

Old Sawmill Cottage
Kilkerran
Maybole
Ayrshire
KA19 7PZ
Bed & Breakfast

Orkney Images
Via House
Sandwick
Stromness
Orkney
KW16 3JF
✆ 01856 841207
📧 via@orkneyimages.com
🌐 www.orkneyimages.com
Retreat House

Penninghame House
Penninghame House
Newton Stewart
DG8 6RD
Own Course Programme

Pluscarden Abbey
Pluscarden
Elgin
Morayshire
IV30 3UA
Retreat House

Quiraing Lodge
Staffin, Portree
Isle of Skye
IV51 9JS
Own Course Programme

Rhanich Sheep Farm
The Rhanich, Edderton
Tain, Ross and Cromarty
IV19 1LG
Bed & Breakfast

Rhu Mhor Guest House
Alma Road
Fort William
Inverness-shire
PH33 6BP
Bed & Breakfast

Other Places and Organisations

The Rossan
Auchencairn
Castle Douglas
Dumfries and Galloway
DG7 1QR
Bed & Breakfast

St Columba Hotel
Isle of Iona, Argyll
PA76 6SL
Bed & Breakfast

St Mary's Mission and Renewal Centre
St Mary's Monastery
Kinnoull
Perth
PH2 7BP
Retreat House

Salisbury Centre
2 Salisbury Road
Edinburgh
EH16 5AB
Own Course Programme

Samye Ling Tibetan Centre
Eskdalemuir
Dumfries and Galloway
DG13 0QL
Own Course Programme

Sonnhalde
East Terrace
Kingussie, Inverness-shire
PH21 1JS
Bed & Breakfast

Suilven
Rhue
Ullapool
Ross and Cromarty
IV26 2TJ
Bed & Breakfast

Tabor Trust Retreat Centre
Key House
High Street
Falkland
Fife
KY7 7BU
Retreat House

Tigh a Gharraidh
Acharn
Aberfeldy
Perthshire
PH15 2HP
Bed & Breakfast

Wheatears
Lumsdaine
Coldingham
Eyemouth
Berwickshire
TD14 5UA
Bed & Breakfast

Whitchester Christian Guest House and Retreat Centre
Borthaugh
Hawick
Roxburghshire
TD9 7LN
℆ 01450 377477
Retreat House

Woodwick House
Woodwick Bay
Evie
Orkney
KW17 2PQ
℆ 01856 751330
Bed & Breakfast

◇ Marygate

◇ The Byre

CARLISLE ■   Brookside ◇
                   ◇ Burnlaw
Eden Green   Nentholme ◇
Edwardene Hotel   ■ NEWCASTLE
Honister House ·····
Skiddaw Street ·····◇
                   ◆◆ **Eastgate 21**
                   ◆ **Lattendales 23**
Brightlife 20   Eller Close ◇
                   How Beck ◇
         ◆   Rydal ◇ ◇ Fawcett Mill Fields
◇ Fernleigh   Beech Tree ◇ ◇ Kirkwood

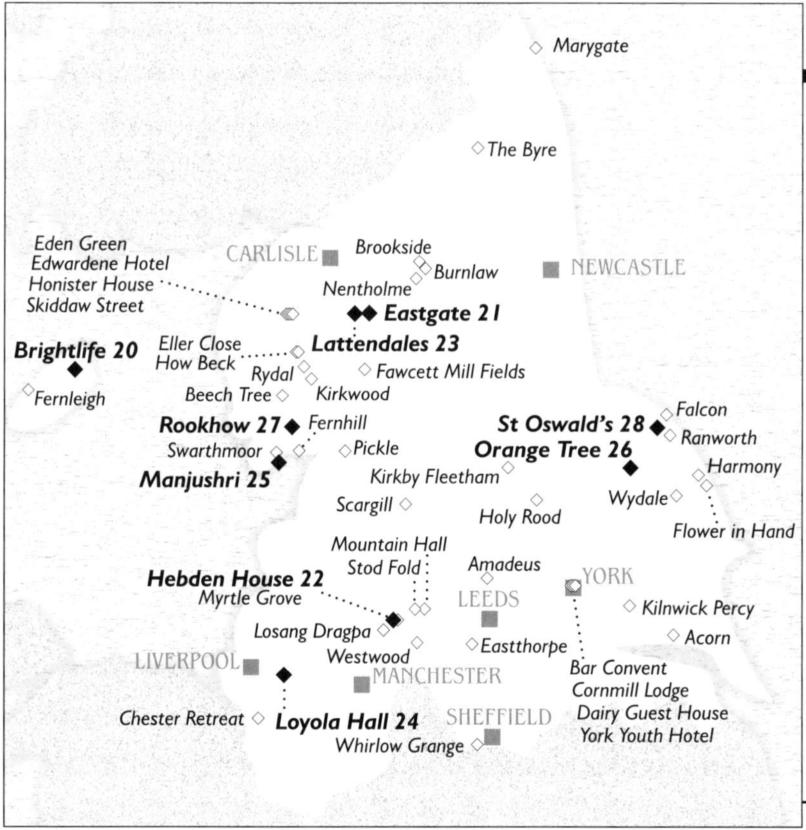

Rookhow 27 ◆ ◇ Fernhill   ◇ Falcon
                                St Oswald's 28 ◆ ◇ Ranworth
Swarthmoor ◇ ◇ Pickle   **Orange Tree 26** ◆
Manjushri 25 ◆   ◇ Harmony
                Kirkby Fleetham ◇   Wydale ◇
        Scargill ◇   ◇
                     Holy Rood ◇   Flower in Hand ◇

        Mountain Hall ◇
        Stod Fold ◇   Amadeus ◇   ◇ YORK
Hebden House 22 ·····   ◇ Kilnwick Percy
Myrtle Grove ·····◇   LEEDS ■
                   ◆ ◇   ◇ Acorn
Losang Dragpa ◇   ◇ Eastthorpe
LIVERPOOL ■   Westwood ◇   Bar Convent
            ◆   ■ MANCHESTER   Cornmill Lodge
Chester Retreat ◇ **Loyola Hall 24** SHEFFIELD ■ Dairy Guest House
            Whirlow Grange ◇   York Youth Hotel

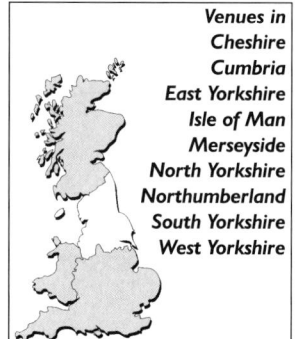

Brightlife

Pam Beldan
Ballalheaney House
Andreas Road
Andreas
Isle of Man
IM7 4EN
© 01624 880318
📠 01624 880967
📧 brightlife@brightlife.com

✔ **Retreat House**
✔ **Own Course Programme**
✔ **Venue for hire**

⚓ 10 double/single rooms, Five diamond, gold crown luxury
🍽 gourmet cuisine
♿ one bedroom disabled adapted
✈ 35 minute plane ride from Liverpool

Focus
Holistic centre for spiritual development

Relax in luxury and discover hidden talents with week-end courses at Brightlife. At the heart of the British Isles, the Isle of Man is an Island steeped in history and rich in Heritage, a mystical place to relax in luxury, enjoy gourmet cuisine and discover hidden talents with weekend workshops and week-long retreats at Brightlife. Set in seclusion and surrounded by the beauties of nature, Brightlife offers you the chance to relax and recharge. There is a unique library of books on personal and spiritual development, also a floatation suite and BETAR sound therapy room.

Brightlife Conferencing offers a bespoke service tailored to your requirements, with the emphasis on attention to detail.

Event Types
Guided group weekend retreats, Business retreats.

Subject Specialities
Personal development, health & healing, spiritual awareness.

Eastgate Barn

Whether you are looking for an inspirational retreat, a 'transformational' holiday, a unique venue for a special occasion or workshop, or simply an idyllic 'Place to Be', Eastgate Barn, as an architect guest says, "..has a rare perfection. It is lovely in every conceivable way."

Nestling at the foot of the Pennines in the lush Eden Valley in Cumbria is the tiny, quintessentially English village of Milburn. A cul-de-sac, with no through traffic, the principal residences surround a village green with its heart, a small but thriving village school.

Eastgate Barn stands on the top fellside of the village, set back from the green, with doors that open onto a track up to the fells, and a 10' picture window with panoramic views of the Lake District. It has been lovingly restored to retain its rustic feel, but with comforts such as underfloor heating.

Rejuvenation of Body, Mind and Spirit

The Barn has been restored with the specific intention of being a place of rest, refreshment and renewal for Body, Mind and Spirit. Hire it for a group, or come to one of the courses we run or host. You may be self-catering, or we can cater for you. Julie teaches the Alexander Technique, and has been working in personal development and spirituality for over 20 years.

Julie Parker
Eastgate Barn
Milburn
Penrith
Cumbria
CA10 1TN
✆ 01768 361509
✉ julie@eastgatebarn.com

✔ **Retreat House**
✔ **Holiday Operator**
✔ **Own Course Programme**
✔ **Venue for hire**
group full board, group self catering, large indoor space

↝ Accommodates 6.
🍽 Special diets catered for.
🚌 Transport possible from local station on request.

Focus
Individual
spirituality

Hebden House

Lynn Prior
The Birchcliffe Centre
Birchcliffe Road
Hebden Bridge
West Yorkshire
HX7 8DG

© 01422 843626
✆ 01422 843648
✉ enqs@hebden-house.co.uk

✔ Venue for hire
group full board (£39.50 to £47), large indoor space, several small spaces
↘ 58 bedspaces (15 singles, 1 twin, 15 family rooms.)
🍽 Non veg as standard, but vegetarian food is our speciality. Special diets catered for.
♿ Wheelchair access to training room and ground floor bedrooms.
🚌 Bus and train.

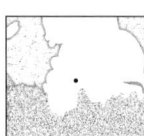

Set in two acres of woodland, Hebden House offers a peaceful and secluded setting from which to run courses, workshops, seminars and retreats. Hebden House offers 58 beds in 15 en-suite rooms. Bed linen service is provided. Seminar room for up to 50, plus break-out room and kitchenette, pleasant outlook onto a sheltered courtyard. There is an Additional Conference Area available for up to 400 people. Catering is provided by Jim and Ash from "Laughing Gravy". Vegan food a speciality of the chefs. Other diets easily catered for. Separate dining room seats 58. Disabled toilets and Stannah lifts to all levels. Youth groups must be supervised.

Event Types
Self directed retreats, business retreats.

Suitability or Specialism
Adults, young people 12 to 17, children under 12

Lattendales

The Friends Fellowship of Healing was formed in 1935 by some members of the Religious Society of Friends (Quakers). The Fellowship believes that God's purpose for humankind is wholeness of body, mind and spirit. It facilitates a number of activities to help people towards achieving this "wholeness". The function of Lattendales is to provide a sanctuary or retreat for those who feel in need of rest, whether spiritually, mentally or physically.

Lattendales is run in accordance with the principles of the Religious Society of Friends, but welcomes everyone irrespective of their religious beliefs.

The house is open from March to November, and guests are invited to enjoy the peaceful atmosphere of Lattendales and its beautiful formal gardens.

Event Types
Self directed retreats.

Subject Specialities
Health & healing, meditation, prayer.

Suitability or Specialism
Adults, couples, women, men, young people 12 to 17, older people.

Nicola Harvey
Lattendales, Berrier Road
Greystoke, Penrith
Cumbria
CA11 0UE
✆ 01768 483229
✆ 01768 483058
✇ wardens@lattendales.info
✔ **Retreat House**
✔ **Bed & Breakfast**
✔ **Own Course Programme**
✔ **Venue for hire**
group full board (£43), group self catering, large indoor space
⌁ 21 bedspaces (5 singles, 7 twins, 1 double.)
▣ Special diets.
♿ 1 twin-bedded room, own toilet.
 Penrith Station then bus or taxi (5 miles)
Focus
Quaker/Open

Loyola Hall

Loyola Hall
Warrington Road
Rainhill
Prescot
Merseyside
L35 6NZ

© 0151 426 4137
✆ 0151 431 0115
✆ mail@loyolahall.co.uk

✔ **Retreat House**
🛏 50 bedspaces (45 singles.)
🍽 Special diets.
♿ All public areas of house are wheelchair accessible
🚆 Train to Rainhill Station or bus 61/161 from Runcorn or Liverpool

Focus Ignatian spirituality

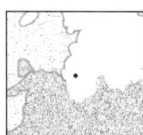

Loyola Hall is a centre of Ignatian spirituality, run in the Roman Catholic tradition, maintained by the Society of Jesus (the Jesuits), and welcoming Christians of all denominations as well as those of other faiths or who have no religious affiliation. As a retreat centre we are open for those who need space in a busy life, those who seek to get in touch with themselves and with the God who enables them to build up God's Kingdom. We strive to ensure that the Centre is a safe, welcoming, relaxing and non-judgemental place where all can feel respected and accepted.

Centre facilities

Opened in 1923, the Centre is situated in large, beautiful grounds near Rainhill vil-

lage between Liverpool and Manchester. It has a modern prayerful chapel, many smaller prayer rooms, two spacious conference rooms, an art

room, lounges, and a number of other meeting rooms. There is also a leisure room with sauna, Jacuzzi and some simple exercise machines. All accommodation is in recently renovated single en-suite bedrooms. All public areas of the house are wheelchair-accessible.

Programme

We offer a year-round programme of individually-guided, themed and preached retreats (many in silence), as well as training courses in Ignatian spirituality. New this year: Rest & Relaxation retreats. There are also day events for individuals, families, and those involved in Christian ministry. Both our web-site and the printed programme (available on request) give more details of all of these.

Manjushri Kadampa Meditation Centre

Manjushri Kadampa Meditation Centre, based at Conishead Priory in Ulverston, provides an inspiring and peaceful environment in which people can learn about Buddhism and meditation.

Manjushri Centre offers a wide variety of courses on meditation and Buddhist practices which are suitable for everyone, from those who seek simple relaxation to those who wish to find lasting inner peace and contentment through following the Buddhist path.

In the grounds of Manjushri Centre is the beautiful Kadampa World Peace Temple, which was built by the Buddhist community to prove a place for quiet reflection and spiritual inspiration. Prayers are held daily in the Temple as well as regular weekend courses. Just south of the Lake District, Conishead Priory is beautifully situated in many acres of woodland and gardens on the shores of Morecambe Bay. The beach is only a five minute walk from the Priory through mature woodland which provides a quiet and reflective environment.

If you would like to find out more about Manjushri Centre and the courses and study programmes we offer, or would like to do a working visit and spend time as part of our community please call or visit our website.

Conishead Priory
Ulverston
Cumbria
LA12 9QQ

℡ 01229 584029
℻ 01229 584029
⌨ info@manjushri.org

✔ **Retreat House**
✔ **Own Course Programme**
🍽 Exclusively vegetarian.

Focus Buddhist

The Orange Tree

http://www.theorangetree.com

Rob Davies, The Orange Tree
Rosedale Abbey, Rosedale East
Pickering, North Yorkshire
YO18 8RH

© 01751 417219
✆ 01751 417219
✎ relax@theorangetree.com

✔ **Retreat House**
✔ **Holiday Operator**
✔ **Own Course Programme**
✔ **Venue for hire**

group full board (£75 to £100), large indoor space
↪ 17 bedspaces (1 single, 7 twins, 1 double, 1 triple)
🍽 Excl vegtrn, special diets.
♿ Wheelchair access: 2 beds on ground floor plus guests lounge and dining room.
🚌 Nearest bus station:

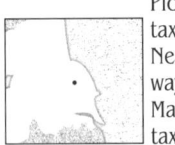

Pickering, then taxi (20 min). Nearest railway station: Malton, then taxi (35 min).

The Orange Tree is a 4 diamond, family run "Relaxation Centre" situated in a beautiful, tranquil location in Rosedale, deep in the heart of the North Yorkshire Moors. We run "Relaxation Weekends" throughout the year, accommodating up to 17 people, combining great vegi food and wine with two relaxation sessions, a choice of treatments, sauna and lovely walks straight out of the front door.

Our mainly ensuite rooms are all comfortably furnished and we encourage informality – it's just a home from home.

We accept bookings in any combination from 1 to 17 people, with no single supplement. We charge £159 per person which includes two nights, all meals and 2 relaxation sessions.

Perhaps the most beautifully situated budget accommodation in the Lake District; in 14 acres of peaceful woodland, between Coniston Water and Windermere. By Grizedale Forest, with its sculpture and trails. Stunning walking/biking country. Rookhow is an early 'Quaker' or 'Friends' Meeting House. The Centre provides accommodation in the former stables. Lovely new woodstove installed in lounge/kitchen/dining room. Self-catering, though catering can sometimes be arranged. The Meeting House, in use since 1725, is available separately for conferences, workshops, seminars, dance, yoga etc. Open to those of all denominations or of none. Bedspaces from £11 per person per night, £6 junior. Twenty bedspaces, extra with camping. Spiritual retreats of all kinds.

Event Types
Guided group retreats, self directed retreats, business retreats, working holidays.

Subject Specialities
Arts & crafts, conservation work, outdoor activities & sport, body & breathwork, meditation.

Eco-tourism features
12 acres of woods managed ecologically. Camping option.

Robert Straughton
Rookhow Centre
Rusland
Ulverston
Cumbria
LA12 8LA

© 01229 860231
℡ 01229 860231
✆ rookhow@britishlibrary.net

✔ **Retreat House**
✔ **Venue for hire**
group self catering, large indoor space, several small spaces
⌨ 20 bedspaces.
🚃 Train to Grange Over Sands or Ulverston then taxi.

Focus
Quaker (all welcome)

St Oswald's Pastoral Centre

St Oswald's, Woodlands Drive,
Sleights, Whitby
North Yorkshire YO21 1RY
© 01947 810496
☏ 01947 810750
✉ ohpstos@globalnet.co.uk
✔ **Retreat House**
✔ **Own Course Programme**
✔ **Venue for hire**
group full board, large indoor space, several small spaces
☞ 17 bedspaces (10 singles, 3 twins.)
🍽 Special diets.
♿ Wheelchair access to one single room.
🚆 Train to Sleights Station or coach from York to Sleights bridge. 15 min walk or we can meet. Also bus from Scarborough to Whitby then taxi.

Focus
Christian/
Anglican

St Oswald's Pastoral Centre is run by four Sisters of the Anglican Order of the Holy Paraclete. Within the context of our regular rhythm of prayer and worship, we offer hospitality to individuals or small groups for retreat, rest or quiet. The Centre is situated

in its own grounds overlooking the Esk valley and the North York Moors. It is an ideal centre for those who enjoy walking and is three miles from the historic port and town of Whitby with its Abbey ruins and picturesque harbour. Guests are welcome to join

the Sisters for services and Sisters can be available by pre-arrangement if anyone wants a listening ear, pastoral support or some guidance on making a retreat.

The Grimston Room is a large conference room which is available for day groups of up to 40. The Centre runs a programme of events through the year.

Normally the Centre is closed on Sunday nights.

The order also runs the nearby Sneaton Castle Centre: see www.sneatoncastle.com

Event Types
Guided group retreats, guided individual retreats, self directed retreats, own course programme.

Subject Specialities
Prayer.

Suitability or Specialism
Adults, couples, older people.

Other Places and Organisations

Acorn Guest House
719 Beverley High Road
Hull, East Yorkshire
HU6 7JN
Bed & Breakfast

Amadeus Vegetarian Hotel
115 Franklin Road
Harrogate, North Yorkshire
HG1 5EN
Bed & Breakfast

The Bar Convent
17 Blossom Street
York YO24 1AQ
Bed & Breakfast

Beech Tree Guest House
Yewdale Road
Coniston, Cumbria
LA21 8DX
Bed & Breakfast

Brookside House
Town Foot, Haltwhistle
Northumberland
NE49 0ER
Bed & Breakfast

Burnlaw Healing and Retreat Centre
Burnlaw, Whitfield
Northumberland
NE47 8HF
Retreat House

The Byre Vegetarian B&B
Harbottle, Morpeth
Northumberland
NE65 7DG
Bed & Breakfast

Chester Retreat House
11 Abbey Square
Chester CH1 2HU
Retreat House

Cornmill Lodge
120 Haxby Road
York YO31 8JP
Bed & Breakfast

Dairy Guest House
3 Scrarcroft Road
York
YO23 1ND
Bed & Breakfast

Eastthorpe Holistic Health Spa
Eastthorpe House
Mirfield, West Yorkshire
WF14 8AE
Health Spa

Eden Green
20 Blencathra Street
Keswick, Cumbria
CA12 4HP
Bed & Breakfast

Edwardene Hotel
26 Southey Street
Keswick, Cumbria
CA12 4EB
Bed & Breakfast

Eller Close
Grasmere, Ambleside
Cumbria LA22 9RW
Bed & Breakfast

Other Places and Organisations

Falcon Guest House
29 Falcon Terrace
Whitby, North Yorkshire
YO21 1EH
℡ 01947 603507
Bed & Breakfast

Fawcett Mill Fields
Gaisgill, Tebay
Penrith, Cumbria CA10 3UB
Venue for hire

**Fernhill Vegetarian
Country House**
Witherslack, Grange-over-
Sands, Cumbria LA11 6RX
Bed & Breakfast

Fernleigh Hotel
Marine Parade
Peel, Isle of Man
IM5 1PB
Bed & Breakfast

The Flower in Hand
Burr Bank
Scarborough
North Yorkshire
YO11 1PN
Bed & Breakfast

Harmony Country Lodge
Limestone Road
Burniston
Scarborough
North Yorkshire
YO13 0DG
℡ 0800 298 5840
Retreat House

Holy Rood House
10 Sowerby Road
Thirsk
North Yorkshire
YO7 1HX
Retreat House

Honister House
1 Borrowdale Road
Keswick, Cumbria
CA12 5DD
Bed & Breakfast

How Beck
Grasmere, Ambleside
Cumbria, LA22 9RH
Bed & Breakfast

Kilnwick Percy Hall
Kilnwick Percy Hall
Pocklington
York
YO4 2UF
Own Course Programme

Kirkby Fleetham Hall
Kirkby Fleetham
Northallerton
DL7 0SU
Venue for hire

Kirkwood Guest House
Princes Road
Windermere
Cumbria
LA23 2DD
Bed & Breakfast

**Losang Dragpa
Buddhist Centre**
Dobroyd Castle
Pexwood Road
Todmorden
OL14 7JJ
*Own Course
Programme*

Marygate House
Holy Island
Berwick-upon-Tweed
Northumberland
TD15 2SD
Retreat House

Other Places and Organisations

Mountain Hall Centre
Brighouse & Denholme Road
Queensbury, Bradford
West Yorkshire BD13 1LH
Own Course Programme

Myrtle Grove
Old Lees Road, Hebden Bridge
West Yorkshire HX7 8HL
Bed & Breakfast

**Nentholme Vegetarian
Guest House**
The Butts, Alston
Cumbria CA9 3JQ
Bed & Breakfast

Pickle Country House
Pickle Farm, Hutton Roof
Kirkby Lonsdale
Cumbria
LA6 2PH
Bed & Breakfast

**Ranworth Vegetarian
Guesthouse**
Ranworth, Church Road
Ravenscar, Scarborough
North Yorkshire
YO13 0LZ
Bed & Breakfast

Rydal Hall
Ambleside, Cumbria
LA22 9LX
Retreat House

Scargill House
Kettlewell, Skipton
North Yorkshire
BD23 5HU
Venue for hire

32 Skiddaw Street
Keswick, Cumbria
CA12 4BY
Bed & Breakfast

Stod Fold Barn
Stod Fold
Ogden
Halifax
West Yorkshire
HX2 8XL
© 01422 244854
Venue for hire

Swarthmoor Hall
Ulverston
Cumbria
LA12 0JQ
*Own
Course
Programme*

**Westwood Christian
Centre**
Westwood Edge Road
Golcar, Huddersfield
West Yorkshire
HD7 4JY
Venue for hire

**Whirlow Grange Diocesan
Conference Centre**
Eccleshall Road South
Sheffield
South Yorkshire
S11 9PZ
Venue for hire

Wydale Hall
Wydale Lane
Brompton by Sawdon
Scarborough
North Yorkshire
YO13 9DG
Venue for hire

York Youth Hotel
11/13 Bishophill Senior
York
YO1 6EF
Bed & Breakfast

East of England

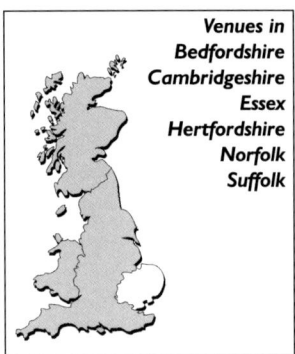

◇ Marsh Barn

◇ Voewood

◇ Old Red Lion

NORWICH ■

◇ Greenbanks

◇ Stockyard Farm

◆ All Hallows 33

◇ Bishop Woodford

St Clarets 34 ◆ ◇ Houghton Chapel

◇ Turvey Abbey

◇ Burwell ◇ Vajrasana

◇ Old Stable House

Dykelands ◈

◇ Ickwell Bury

CAMBRIDGE

◇ Marshwinds

◇ Shrubland

■ LUTON

◇ Western House

◇ Amaravati

◇ Arthur Findlay

◇ All Saints

◇ Bradwell Othona

◇ Beckneywood

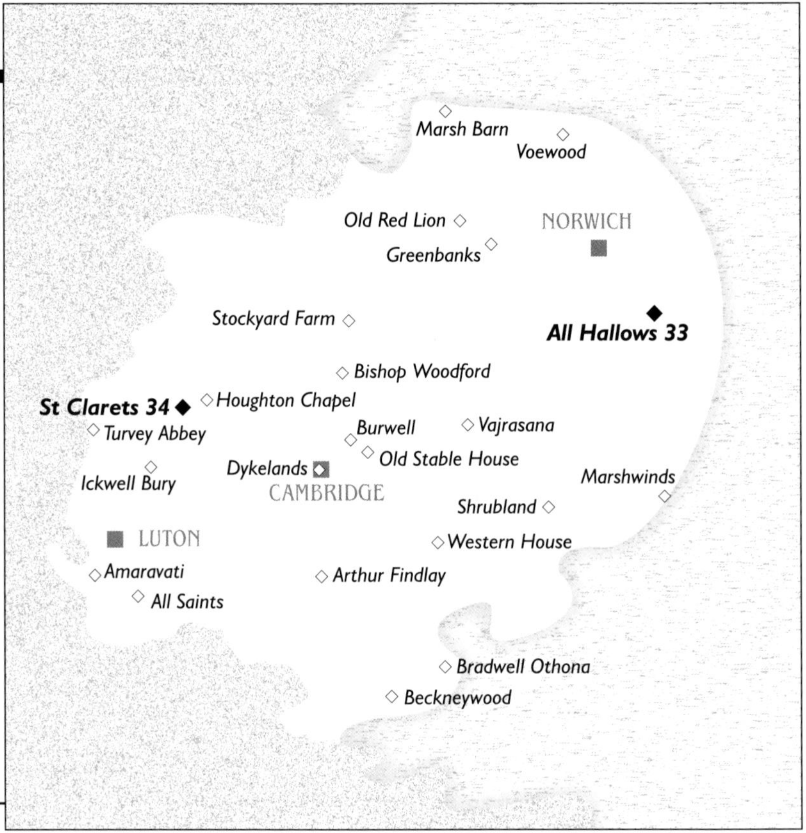

http://www.all-hallows.org.uk

Group bookings, conferences, retreats, parish and youth groups catered for. Set within beautiful countryside. Tennis courts and an outside pool are on site. Midweek reductions available.

St Gabriel's Conference Centre can accommodate up to 100+ in various single, twin and family rooms, some en suite. **St Michael's Retreat House** has 16 single and 4 twin. Both are full board. Venue hire costs £28.50 to £42.50 per person for overnight stays, and £8.50 to £14 per person for day groups, including lunch.

Individual Retreat at St Mary's Lodge

A silent retreat house on the Norfolk/Suffolk border, where the atmosphere and surroundings are conductive to reflection, study, prayer, solitude and rest. A library, art room and Chapel are available for visitors to use. Self-catering. Rooms: 2 flats, 3 bedsitting rooms.

Individual Retreat at All Hallows House

A pleasant retreat house offering rest and relaxation in the comfortable surroundings. There are two sitting rooms and a spacious garden with summerhouse. Suitable for family holidays and individual short breaks. Full Board.

Rooms: 4 single, 2 twin.

Individual Retreat at Holy Cross House.

The guest wing of the Convent, offering rest, quiet and private retreat. Accommodation is full board; breakfast and supper are provided in the dinning room and the midday meal is taken with the Sisters, usually in silence. The house is within easy reach of the Convent Chapel, and guests are welcome to join the Sisters for prayer and worship. Rooms: 10 single.

Individual Retreat at All Hallows House, Norwich

Available for rest, quiet and private retreat. An oasis situated amongst city activity. Next to the shrine of Julian of Norwich. Rooms: 2 single, 2 twin.

Address: Rouen Road, Norwich NRI IQT. 01603 624738

Community of All Hallows
Ditchingham
Bungay
Suffolk
NR35 2DT

℅ 01986 892749
℅ 01986 895838
℅ secretary@allhallowsconvent.fsbusiness.co.uk

✔ **Retreat House**
✔ **Own Course Programme**
✔ **Venue for hire**
group full board (£28.50 to £42.50), large indoor space, several small spaces
↝ 120 bedspaces.
🍽 Special diets.
🚆 Taxi from Beccles Railway Station or bus from Norwich.

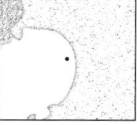

Focus Church of England
– All welcome

St Claret Centre

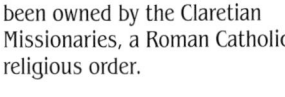

Father Paul Smyth
The Towers, High Street
Buckden, Huntingdon
PE19 5TA
✆ 01480 811284
✆ 01480 811918
✍
claret-centre@cmfbuck.force9.net
✔ **Retreat House**
✔ **Bed & Breakfast**
✔ **Own Course Programme**
✔ **Venue for hire**
group full board & self catering
⌒ 13 twins & 2 sing, B&B or
full-board. Inner Gatehouse: 4
apartments, full-board, B&B
or self-catering. Great Tower:
2 dorms sleeping total of 40
(4 singles for group leaders).
♿ Twin-bedded room adapted
for wheelchair users.

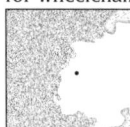 🚆 Train to
Huntingdon or
St Neots then
bus, car or
taxi

Set in its own 15 acre estate, the Claret Centre offers seclusion and tranquillity at an accessible location. Between the 12th and 15th centuries the site was developed into an ecclesiastical palace by successive Bishops of Lincoln. Several buildings from this time have survived and have

recently been restored, including the Great Tower and the Inner Gatehouse. In the 1870s the estate passed out of ecclesiastical ownership and a mansion house was added to the older buildings on the site. This splendid house now forms the core of the Claret Centre. Since the 1950s the estate has

been owned by the Claretian Missionaries, a Roman Catholic religious order.

Retreats and Course Programme
The facilities can be hired by groups and individuals of all faiths or none, for self-directed retreats, courses or holidays with no input from the resident community. Alternatively, members of the pastoral team offer programmes designed for young people as well as residential and day events for adults.

Facility Hire
Meeting rooms located in the Main House and the Great Tower can be hired. The St Claret chapel is also available for the use of visitors. Particularly suitable for Adults and older children.

Other Places and Organisations

All Saints Pastoral Centre
London Colney
St Albans
Hertfordshire
AL2 1AF
Venue for hire

Amaravati Buddhist Centre
Great Gaddesden
Hemel Hempstead
Hertfordshire
HP1 3BZ
Retreat House

The Arthur Findlay College
Stansted Hall
Church Road, Burton End
Stansted, Essex
CM24 8UD
Own Course Programme

Beckneywood House
Lower Road
Hockley
Essex
SS5 5LD
Bed & Breakfast

Bishop Woodford House
Barton Road
Ely, Cambridgeshire
CB7 4DX
Retreat House

Bradwell Othona Community
East Hall Farm
East End Road
Bradwell on Sea
Southminster
Essex
CM0 7PN
Retreat House

Burwell House
North Street
Burwell
Cambridge
CB5 0BA
Venue for hire

Dykelands Guesthouse
157 Mowbray Road
Cambridge
CB1 7SP
Bed & Breakfast

Greenbanks Hotel
Swaffham Road
Wendling
Dereham
Norfolk
NR19 2AB
Bed & Breakfast

Houghton Chapel Centre
Church View
Chapel Lane
Houghton
Huntingdon
Cambridgeshire
PE17 2AY
Venue for hire

Ickwell Bury
Biggleswade
Bedfordshire
SG18 9EF
Own Course Programme

Other Places and Organisations

Marsh Barn
Deepdale Farm
Burnham Deepdale
Kings Lynn, Norfolk
PE31 8DD
Venue for hire

Marshwinds
32 Saxmundham Road
Aldeburgh, Suffolk
IP15 5JE
Bed & Breakfast

The Old Red Lion
Bailey Street
Castle Acre
Kings Lynn
Norfolk
PE32 2AG
© 01760 755557
Bed & Breakfast

The Old
Stable House Centre
3 Sussex Lodge
Fordham Road
Newmarket
Suffolk
CB8 7AF
Venue for hire

Shrubland Hall
Coddenham
Ipswich
Suffolk
IP6 9QH
Health Spa

Stockyard Farm B&B
Wisbech Road
Welney
Wisbech
Cambridgeshire
PE14 9RQ
Bed & Breakfast

Turvey Abbey
Turvey
Bedford
MK43 8DE
Retreat House

Vajrasana Retreat Centre
care of
London Buddhist Centre
51 Roman Road
Bethnal Green, London
E2 0HU
Retreat House

Voewood
Cromer Road
High Kelling
Holt
Norfolk
NR25 6QS
Venue for hire

Western House
High Street
Cavendish
Sudbury
Suffolk
CO10 8AR
Bed & Breakfast

Unstone Grange 42

◇ Edward King

Atlow Mill

NOTTINGHAM

◇

The Grange 38

Morley ◇

◆ **Time Away 41**

Anson's Place

Tara Centre ◇

Darby House

Hoar Cross ◇

Igloo Backpackers

Mynd House

◇

LEICESTER

◇ Parkdale

Oak Barn ◇

Woodbrooke 43 ◆ BIRMINGHAM

◇ Launde Abbey

Bramlea

Offa House

◇

◇

Bredwardine

◇ Old Country

Eirene Centre

◇

◇

Canon Frome

Haie Barn

◇ Parkfield

◆

Poulstone Court 40

Holycombe 39

◆

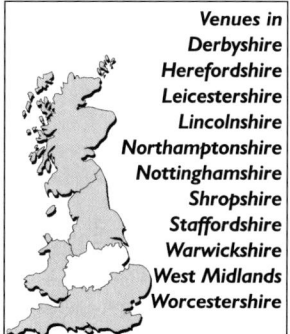

Venues in
Derbyshire
Herefordshire
Leicestershire
Lincolnshire
Northamptonshire
Nottinghamshire
Shropshire
Staffordshire
Warwickshire
West Midlands
Worcestershire

PLACES **TO BE**

The Grange

Rosie Ward-Allen
The Grange, Grange Road
Ellesmere, Shropshire
SY12 9DE
© 01691 623495
✆ 01691 623227
✉ rosie@thegrange.uk.com

✔ **Own Course Programme**
✔ **Venue for hire**
group full board (£44 to £54), large indoor space, several small spaces
⤳ 25 bedspaces (5 singles, 4 twins, 4 doubles, 2 family rooms, most with en-suite bathrooms.)
🍽 Special diets.
♿ Wheelchair access.
🚌 Shrewsbury Station then bus or taxi (approximately 45 minutes travelling time)
Focus
Open-minded

Set in 10 beautiful acres of lawns, woodland, organic herb and vegetable gardens, and with light and large public lounges and library, there is plenty of scope at the Grange for individuals and groups to find their own quiet spaces and peaceful surroundings.

We have our own programme of events that includes art and craft workshops, yoga, meditation, and exploring the second half of life for women. We also take block bookings from groups looking for venues. Believing that there are many routes to spiritual peace and

fulfilment, we are open minded about the religious backgrounds, or not, of our guests, welcoming all. The Grange is just outside the small town of Ellesmere, located in a wonderfully unspoilt region of north Shropshire, justly called the Shropshire lakeland, and is in striking distance of the magnificent Welsh borderlands.

Event Types
Guided group retreats, business retreats, own course programme.

Subject Specialities
Arts & crafts, body & breathwork, inner process, meditation, outdoor activities & sport, prayer, self expression.

Suitability or Specialism
Adults.

Holycombe

Holycombe is a haven for peace, healing and joyful activities where music, dance song, play, meditation, bodywork and healing can renew energy and well-being. Set in a verdant wooded valley on the edge of the Cotswold village of Whichford, Andy and Sally Birtwell have built a beautiful house to honour the sacred landscape, which was once a Norman castle with a moat that still remains. Using ecological and geomantic principles they have created a space where facilitators can bring their residential groups (18 maximum) and enjoy stunning workshop space and 6 acres of garden that include a pond, moat, stone circle, shady coppice, fire-pit, barbecue, grass tennis court, hot tub and space for sweat lodge and camping. There are also regular weekday dance, yoga, and t'ai chi classes, and other weekend events. Various therapies are available during the week. We also have a self-catered retreat flat to let for long weekends with the ancient Whichford Wood just across the fields, and of course, the Rollright Stones nearby. There is a pottery in the village, and pub. Stratford-upon-Avon, Oxford, Chipping Campden and the stunning golden Cotswold villages are a short drive away. We charge £33 per person per 24 hours for the residential workshop accommodation. We can put you in touch with a caterer or you can self-cater. You bring your own bed linen and towels. We welcome woofers. All info on the website – we do not have a brochure.

Eco-tourism features

House built using all eco or recycled products, in process of using grey water and plan heat pump. Historic site of Whichford Castle with moat, stone circle and labyrinth.

Sally Birtwell, Holycombe
Whichford, Shipston-on-Stour
Warwickshire, CV36 5PH
℡ 01608 684239
℡ 01608 684501
✉ sally@holycombe.com

✔ **Retreat House**
✔ **Own Course Programme**
✔ **Venue for hire**
group self catering (£33 to £38), large indoor space, several small spaces
⌁ 18 bedspaces (1 room sleeps 6 plus, other 6 rooms can be used as singles, twins, doubles)
🍽 A caterer can be provided.
🚌 Train to Banbury or Moreton-in-Marsh then taxi. Bus to Chipping Norton, Shipston-on-Stour then taxi.

Focus Honour all paths and spiritual traditions

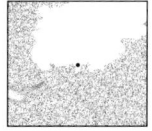

Poulstone Court

http://www.poulstone.com

Poulstone Court
Kings Caple
Hereford
HR1 4UA

✆ 01432 840251
✆ 01432 840860
✆ poulstone@btinternet.com

✔ Venue for hire
group full board, large indoor space
⛵ 36 bedspaces.
🍽 Special diets.
🚉 Hereford railway station 6 miles.

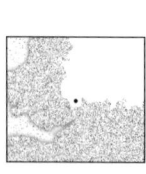

Poulstone Court, a spacious and comfortable Victorian country house, is a residential venue midway between Hereford and Ross-on-Wye. Five minutes' walk from the River Wye, it lies in lush, peaceful surroundings. The beautiful grounds include a walled garden and flat lawns perfect for outside activity. Sleeping accommodation is in attrac-

tively furnished one- to five-bedded rooms, with a self-contained flat ideal for facilitators. Two large workshop spaces in the house are complemented by a spacious barn, perfect for movement. All food is vegetarian. Poulstone Court is regularly used for courses in T'ai Chi, meditation, healing, counselling, shamanism, yoga and movement. We specialise in creating a clear, vibrant space consecrated to service, nourishment and support for the groups and courses that come here.

Event Types
Regeneration programmes.

Subject Specialities
Body & breathwork, health & healing, inner process, ritual & shamanic, meditation, T'ai Chi, Yoga.

Suitability or Specialism
Adults.

Enjoy Time Away at Station House, situated in the heart of rural Lincolnshire, overlooking the River Witham and giving views of the surrounding countryside in all directions. We feel we can share our house, which is spacious, comfortable and quietly situated, with people who are looking for an atmosphere somewhere between a holiday guest-house and a retreat-house.

Our aim is to provide a supportive, caring and peaceful environment for people needing a period of recuperation after a difficult time or for those who need time just to sit and reflect and be – we can remove the responsibilities of everyday life for a short while and give time and space to our guests.

The house and signal box, built by the Great Northern Railway in the nineteenth century, have been joined and extended to provide three day rooms (two overlook the river) and three en-suite bedrooms. Three acres of garden and woodland give guests ample space to

walk or sit outdoors and the former railway track provides scope for further walking and the study and appreciation of local flora and fauna.

People of all ages, all faiths and denominations (and none) are welcome.

Graham and Valerie Byers
Station House
Station Road
Stixwould
Woodhall Spa
Lincolnshire
LN10 5HW
© 01526 352548
timeaway@stixwold.surfaid.org

✔ **Retreat House**
✔ **Bed & Breakfast**
✔ **Venue for hire**
group full board (up to £35)
⤵ 6 bedspaces (3 twins)
🍽 Special diets.
♿ Ramps to 2 outer doors, 2 ground floor bedrooms, stairlift available.
🚌 Coach to Woodhall Spa or train to Lincoln, Boston or Sleaford. We will collect from stations.

Unstone Grange

Unstone Grange
Crow Lane
Unstone
Dronfield
Derbyshire
S18 4AL

© 01246 412344
📞 01246 412344
🖐

admin@unstonegrange.co.uk

✔ Venue for hire

group full board, group self catering, large indoor space, several small spaces

↝ 35 bedspaces (4 twins, 6 family rooms.)

🍽 Special diets.

🚆 Chesterfield Station

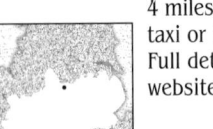

4 miles, take taxi or buses. Full details at website.

Focus Open

A centre for personal creative growth. Set in the lovely Derbyshire countryside, the atmosphere at Unstone Grange attracts community and youth groups of all types. They come to use our centre to access and express their creative spirit through dance, drama, craft-work, writing, painting, music, meditation, bodywork, healing and a wide range of other activities. From £13 per person per night self catering. Unstone Grange is owned by the Unstone Grange Trust, whose aim is to hold and main-tain the place for use by community groups of all kinds who are in accord with our underlying ethos of unity in diversity. Groups booking the house have sole use of it whatever their size (subject to a minimum of 15 at weekends). This means that we are not usually able to accommodate people who are looking for an individual retreat place. The barn is available either as a separate non-residential space or in addition to the house as a larger meeting space. For larger groups we have camp-ing space, and sometimes land is available to hire from our neighbour for extra tents or parking. Check our website for availability, booking forms, charges, directions and a host of other information.

Event Types

Guided group retreats, self directed retreats, working holidays.

Subject Specialities

Alternative lifestyles & technology, arts & crafts, body & breathwork, conservation work, counselling, earth mysteries, food & gardening, group process, health & healing, inner process, meditation, prayer, ritual & shamanic.

Suitability or Specialism

Adults.

Eco-tourism features

Over 2 acres of organic gardens and orchards. Soil Association certified.

Woodbrooke Quaker Study Centre

Woodbrooke, set in its own 10 acres of organically managed garden and grounds, provides a refreshing oasis of calm in an urban setting. The house is a handsome Grade 2 listed building given to the Religious Society of Friends by the famous chocolate maker, George Cadbury, in 1903.

We provide comfortable hospitality as well as delicious food, catering for a range of special diets.There are several meeting rooms, the largest accommodating up to 100 people. Additionally an open access library and art room are available for guests' use. The day begins and ends with a period of worship that is open to all who wish to attend.

The atmosphere is special and all who work here want guests to use make the most of Woodbrooke to enhance their own work and lives.

Please call us to receive a copy of our bi-annual course brochure.

Eco-tourism features

Set in Birmingham's largest organically managed garden.

1046 Bristol Road
Birmingham
West Midlands
B29 6LJ

℃ 0121 472 5171
📠 0121 472 5173
📧 enquiries@woodbrooke.org.uk

✔ **Own Course Programme**
✔ **Venue for hire**
group full board, large indoor space, several small spaces
🍽 Special diets.
🚌 Lots of regular buses from Birmingham New Street station or local train to Selly Oak.

Focus Quaker

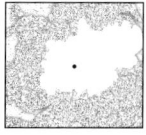

Other Places and Organisations

Anson's Place
21 Waverley Avenue
Gedling
Nottingham
NG4 3HH
Bed & Breakfast

Bramlea Bed & Breakfast
Barons Cross Road
Leominster
Herefordshire
HR6 8RW
Bed & Breakfast

Darby House
10 The Grove
Southey Street
Nottingham
NG7 4BQ
Bed & Breakfast

Haie Barn Vegetarian B&B
The Bage
Dorstone
Hereford
HR3 5SU
© 01497 831729
Bed & Breakfast

Atlow Mill Centre for Emotional Education
Atlow Mill
Hognaston
Ashbourne
Derbyshire
DE6 1PX
© 01335 370494
Own Course Programme

Bredwardine Lodge
Bredwardine
Hereford
HR3 6BZ
Bed & Breakfast

Edward King House
The Old Palace
Minster Yard
Lincoln
LN2 1PU
Bed & Breakfast

Playroom at Canon Frome
Canon Frome
Ledbury
Herefordshire
HR8 2TD
Venue for hire

The Eirene Centre
The Old School
Clopton
Kettering
Northamptonshire
NN14 3DZ
Venue for hire

Hoar Cross Hall
Hoar Cross
Lichfield
Staffordshire
DE13 8QS
Retreat House

Other Places and Organisations

Igloo Backpackers Hostel
110 Mansfield Road
Nottingham
NG1 3HL
Bed & Breakfast

Launde Abbey
East Norton, Leicester
LE7 9XB
Retreat House

Morley Retreat & Conference House
Church Lane, Morley
Ilkeston, Derbyshire
DE7 6DE
Retreat House

Mynd House
Ludlow Road, Little Stretton
Church Stretton, Shropshire
SY6 6RB
Bed & Breakfast

Oak Barn Workshops
Nordybank Nurseries
Clee St Margaret, Craven Arms
Shropshire SY7 9DT
Venue for hire

Offa House – Coventry Diocesan Retreat & Conference Centre
Offchurch, Leamington Spa
Warwickshire CV33 9AS
℡ 01926 423309
Retreat House

Old Country House
Mathon
Malvern
Worcestershire
WR13 5PS
℡ 01886 880867
Bed & Breakfast

Parkdale Yoga Centre
10 Parkdale West
Wolverhampton
West Midlands
WV1 4TE
Retreat House

Parkfield
3 Broad Walk
Stratford upon Avon
Warwickshire
CV37 6HS
Bed & Breakfast

Tara Centre
Ashe Hall, Ash Lane
Etwall, Derby
DE65 6HT
Own Course Programme

Wales

Venues in
Anglesey
Carmarthenshire
Ceredigion
Conwy
Denbighshire
Swansea
Newport
Gwynedd
Pembrokeshire
Powys
Wrexham

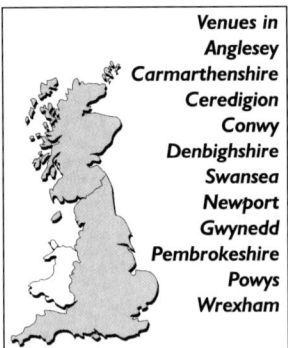

Places to BE 2005/Page 46

Cefn Gribyn ◇
Outdoor Alternative ◇   Plas Madoc
Anglesey Healing 47 ◆
Fort Belan 50 ◆   ◆ **Life Foundation 53**
Trigonos 58   ◇ Hendre
Graianfryn
Snowdon Lodge ◇   Coleg y Groes
Ty'r Ysgol ◇   ◇◇ Vajraloka
Caerwych ◇   Bryn Awel   Fraser Cottage
Ancient Healing Ways   ◇ Taraloka
Hafod
Old Rectory Hotel
Gwalia ◇
Rainbow Rose ◇   ◆ **Spirit Horse 57**
Panteidal ◇
ABERYSTWYTH ■   ◆ **Woodlands 52**
Wilderness Trust
Hillscape ◇   ◇ Cwmllechwedd Fawr
Y Beudy ◇   Cryndir ◇
Old Rectory 55 ◆   ◇ Cwrt Y Cylchau
Dyfed Permaculture   ◆ **Neuadd-Isaf 54**
Mandala ◇
Pen Rhiw 56 ◆   ◇ Trericket Mill
Plas Taliaris ◇
Coleg Trefeca 49 ◆   ◇ Old Post Office
Heartspring 51 ◆   ◇ Llangasty
Ardwyn   ◆
Buckland Hall 48
West Usk Lighthouse
CARDIFF ■   ◇

Anglesey Healing Centre

The Anglesey Healing Centre is situated on the beautiful island of Anglesey between the mountains of Snowdonia and the Irish Sea. We are convenient for the high-speed ferry to Ireland. Close to several beaches, this is a wonderful place to walk, relax, and unwind. The island is rich in Sacred Sites: burial chambers and standing stones. A small family run Centre, we welcome people seeking peace and quiet and an opportunity to go inward, in a healing and spiritual environment.

We offer a self-contained, purpose-built space for personal retreats. Designed for 1 or 2 people, we can accommodate most dietary requirements and the retreat includes all meals and a healing treatment of your choice each day. We run Group Retreats on Bank Holiday weekends, A Course in Miracles Retreats, Meditation and Walking Retreats, and Reiki 1 and 2 classes.

We have an extensive library of New Age books and tapes which guests are welcome to browse, and a beautiful, secluded garden for their pleasure.

Retreats and courses are facilitated by Vivien Candlish, a Reiki Master since 1992, and a Course in Miracles teacher for eight years.

The Centre is warm and comfortable with a welcoming and informal atmosphere.

Event Types
Retreat weekends, Personal retreats, Meditation and Walking Retreats, Reiki 1 and 2 classes, "A Course In Miracles" Retreats, Guided visits to Sacred Sites.

Subject Specialities
Healing, "A Course In Miracles", Spirituality, Meditation, Walking

Suitability or Specialism
Adults

Vivien Candlish
Anglesey Healing Centre
Bro Dawel, Llangoed
Beaumaris, Anglesey
LL58 8PB
℗ 01248 490814
🖳 vivreiki@hotmail.com
✔ **Retreat House**
✔ **Bed & Breakfast**
✔ **Own Course Programme**
↝ Centre: 6 bedspaces.
(2 singles, 2 doubles.)
2 shared bathrooms.
Self-contained Personal Retreat Space: double with bathroom.
🍽 We cater for vegetarians, vegans and meat eaters. Some of the vegetables are from our organic vegetable garden.
🚌 Train or coach to Bangor (North Wales), N57 bus to Glanrafon, or taxi

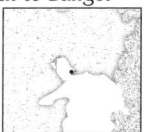

Buckland Hall

Martin Fleming
Buckland Hall, Bwlch
Brecon, Powys
LD3 7JJ
© 01874 730276
✆ 01874 730740
✆ info@bucklandhall.co.uk

✔ **Venue for hire**
group full board (£46 to £68), group self catering, large indoor space, several small spaces
⤳ 68 bedspaces (4 singles, 20 twins, 2 doubles, 5 family rooms.)
🍽 Exclusively vegetarian, special diets.
♿ Wheelchair access, lift to first floor.
🚌 Trains to Abergavenny

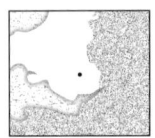

Focus
Supportive, loving energy

Buckland Hall is an amazing space that you can make your own. It is a dedicated venue for all types of group events – whether they are celebrations, courses, retreats and get-togethers. Groups with exclusive use feel they own the place. You have privacy, focus and the opportunity to create the right experience for your session. Buckland Hall is set in 60 acres of gardens and parkland amidst the spectacular Brecon Beacons and overlooking the River Usk. It offers 68 bed spaces in 31 excellent "en-suite" bedrooms. However, since the activity spaces can handle up to 130, many groups use additional local accommodation. Catering is exclusively vegetarian and served in style. Special diets are catered for and groups determine the style of menu and schedule of mealtimes. Access and special bedrooms for disabled needs. Facilities include: large meeting rooms; yoga & meditation room; treatment rooms; snooker & recreation rooms. Registered for weddings.

Event Types
All types of personal growth courses, celebrations, get-togethers, conferences. Detoxification and therapy sessions. Alternative weddings & celebrations.

Suitability or Specialism
Mainly adults and couples, but family groups also welcome.

Eco-tourism features
Spring water, largely organic.

Coleg Trefeca

In the heart of the Brecon Beacons National Park, Coleg Trefeca is a centre for conferences, retreats and lay training. The historic birthplace of Howell Harris, leader of the Methodist Revival in Wales in the 18th century, it is now a listed building, set in 5 acres of grounds. Harris established here a remarkable Christian "family", Teulu Trefeca, which was a virtually self-sufficient community, representing more than 70 different trades and crafts. The College houses a museum including artefacts from the time of Howell Harris. Today the sense of Christian family is still strong. The atmosphere of the house and grounds make this an excellent place to relax, away from day-to-day pressures. Individuals may book into our own course programme, which includes day and residential courses and designated holiday weeks. Please contact us for further details. Groups are welcome to book the centre when available, for their own events.

Event Types
Guided group retreats, own course programme.

Subject Specialities
Prayer, arts & crafts, self expression.

Suitability or Specialism
Adults(++), couples, families with children, older people.

The Warden
Coleg Trefeca, College Lane
Trefeca, Brecon
Powys
LD3 0PP
℡ 01874 711423
✆ 01874 712212
✉ post@trefeca.org.uk
✔ **Bed & Breakfast**
✔ **Own Course Programme**
✔ **Venue for hire**
group full board, large indoor space, several small spaces
↳ 39 bedspaces (18 twins.)
🍽 Special diets.
♿ Wheelchair access.
🚌 Lifts available from Abergavenny (18 miles). A few buses to Talgarth but public transport very limited.

Focus
Christian

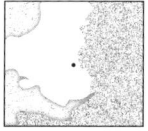

Fort Belan

Llanwnda
Caernarfon, Gwynedd
LL54 5TP
℡ 01286 831350
📠 01286 831350
✉ lynne@fortbelan.co.uk

✔ Retreat House
✔ Venue for hire

group self catering (£16 to £25), large & small spaces

↪ Comfortable self-catering accommodation for up to 40 people in six characterful houses, sleeping from 2 to 12. All fully equipped and centrally heated, most have open fires. Self-contained studio flat ideal base for facilitators. If required, one of the dining rooms can seat up to 28.

♿ Wheelchair access to music room, 3 cottages and courtyard toilet.

🚆 Train to Bangor then 16 mile bus journey. Bus stop is 3 miles from Fort Belan.

Strategically situated on the tip of a private peninsula this Grade 1 listed Napoleonic Fort is flanked by miles of sand dunes and almost deserted beaches with magnificent views across the water to the Snowdonia range of mountains.

Belan is truly unique, as is its beautiful and tranquil location. Its ambience is warm and friendly which helps to promote both relaxation and creativity making it an ideal venue in which to hold your workshop or retreat. It is a lovely place to share a working holiday with your walking or bird watching friends, history society, language class, musical appreciation group, small choir or paint-

ing group etc. Most houses have pianos, and arrangements can be made for use of the magnificent galleried music/lecture room, which holds an audience of up to eighty. All proceeds fund the continuing restoration work.

Outdoor activities

Wonderful walking to suit all levels of fitness.

Bird Watching: Our own 'Bird pack' lists over 200 species seen on the peninsula – maps are included showing the local bird sanctuaries and hides.
Cycling: There is a local Sustrans track.
Fishing: Some of the best sea bass fishing in the UK
Water sports.

Heartspring is surrounded by stunning coastal scenery yet in an easily accessible part of South West Wales. Our grand Victorian house is superbly sited on a hill overlooking a designated Coastal Conservation Area with magnificent views of the beaches, the Norman castle and sleepy untouched village.

What we offer

We offer a tranquil and enriching environment for a relaxing holiday or for Individual retreats and mini-breaks. These can be tailor made to your requirements with the optional addition of complementary therapy and teaching sessions such as Massage, Healing, Profound Relaxation, Meditation and many others from local practitioners.

The house

Heartspring has been lovingly restored with an emphasis on the use of toxic-free environmentally-friendly materials and the rooms are all decorated with natural paints and varnishes. We also have lovely pure spring water for bathing and drinking, and solar heating panels for hot water. All

our meals are fully organic and vegetarian and we offer a fully equipped vegetarian kitchen for those wanting to self-cater.

The house is south facing with large windows to drink in the stunning scenery, and we offer a very peaceful and tranquil atmosphere, free of television and other associated noises.

We have an inspiring environment to help those looking to find their own inner healing, peace and vitality and to let their spirits fly.

Eco-tourism features

Heartspring has been completely renovated using environment-friendly toxic-free materials and paints. We also have solar panels, spring water and serve only organic vegetarian food.

Madeline Lynfield
Hill House
Llansteffan
Carmarthen
SA33 5JG

✆ 01267 241999
🖃 info@heartspring.co.uk

✔ **Retreat House**
✔ **Bed & Breakfast**
🛏 9 beds (1 single, 1 twin, 2 double/family rooms.)
🍽 Exclusively vegetarian, special diets. B&B and half board.
♿ No wheelchair access.
🚌 Bus from Carmarthen to Llansteffan, Sticks Hotel. Steep driveway is after the 4th house beyond the hotel, opposite the church.

Focus

Open to all

Inspiring Breaks

Alan Selkirk
Woodlands
Banhadlog
Llanidloes
Powys
SY18 6JR

✆ 0870 207 0870
✆ 0870 208 0870
🖰

aselkirk@smartsolutions.org.uk

✔ **Retreat House**
✔ **Holiday Operator**
⌁ 2 bedspaces (2 doubles.)
Mainly individual self catering.
Individual B&B (£24 to £29
single, £19 to £24 shared),
no smoking in buildings.
🚗 Collection service from
local station

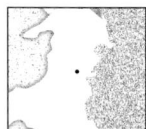

Whether you're looking for inspiration, a healing retreat, or to (re)discover your direction and purpose, here is the near-perfect setting. With panoramic and utterly serene views over thickly wooded valleys and rolling green hills, the house is set in a huge, totally secluded garden and natural woodland, with its own babbling stream and waterfalls feeding four delightful pools. If you spend some time working in the garden or on permaculture design, you could even stay here free! There is a unique library of books on personal and spiritual development, including 35 on the subject of discovering your purpose, vocation and ideal work ... and making a happy living from it! Looking out from the picture window, which captures the morning sun, the sky is decorated with the aerial acrobatics of swallows and hawks, and at the end of a one-mile no-through-road, birdsong is virtually all you will hear! There is a large bathroom with shower and bath and the sitting room contains a very fully equipped kitchenette, spacious writing bureau, and even a Hi-Fi system. The TV may be better used to watch video recordings from a library of hundreds of documentaries, films and comedy/satire programmes. Fresh organic food is available. Within the sheltered 2-acre garden, there are many totally secluded places and a choice of outdoor seats including a hammock. A swinging bench is positioned for the perfect view and the best of the sun, with patio heater for evening stargazing. You can walk directly onto the hills from the top of the garden or enjoy more level walks from the lane, passing rare breed sheep and angora goats. The surrounding area is a special attraction for walkers because of the sheer variety of scenery, and includes the most spectacular section of Offa's Dyke as well as Glyndwr's Way. As well as a table tennis table in the garden, a mountain bike is available with two local dedicated cycle trails and very quiet country lanes. Nearby are places for golfing, swimming, bowling, tennis, squash, and also sailing and angling in the idyllic setting of Lake Clywedog, a haven for rare and migratory birds. Llanidloes has a thriving arts and crafts community and is within easy reach of the Centre for Alternative Technology.

Eco-tourism features
Fresh air heating (heat pump).

Life Foundation – Dru Yoga Centre

The Life Foundation International Course Centre is situated in the beautiful Welsh Mountains of the Snowdonia National Park, North Wales. It is the home of The World Peace Flame, a world-wide peace initiative where seven living flames were lit by peacemakers and united to create 'The World Peace Flame'. For details on this project please go to www.worldpeaceflame.com The Life Foundation is a committed team of individuals from a wide range of backgrounds providing spiritual awareness, self-empowerment, and self-development courses. We teach techniques that integrate the body-heart and mind, creating physical well-being and emotional balance that enables the individual to access their highest potential. We specialise in Dru Yoga and Dru Meditation Teacher Training, weekend Retreats and Spiritual Development Courses. We also take our work into areas of conflict, war zones and decision making arenas throughout the world. "Transform the world by giving people the tools to transform themselves."

Event Types
Own course programme, teacher training.

Subject Specialities
Health & yoga, spiritual self development.

Suitability or Specialism
Adults.

Nant Ffrancon
Bethesda
Bangor
Gwynedd
LL57 3LX

✆ 01248 602900
✆ 01248 602004

enquiries@lifefoundation.org.uk
✔ **Retreat House**
✔ **Bed & Breakfast**
✔ **Holiday Operator**
✔ **Own Course Programme**
⇱ 3 singles, 20 twins.
🍽 Exclusively vegetarian, special diets.
🚌 For international travellers, come to Liverpool or Manchester airports then get a train to Bangor station. The course centre is then an 8 mile taxi ride.

Neuadd-Isaf Farmhouse

Peter and Marie Hill
Lower Hall Stables
Neuadd-Isaf Farm
Maesmynis
Builth Wells
Powys
LD2 3HP

☏ 01982 552479
✉ peter@lowerhall7.fsnet.co.uk

✔ **Retreat House**
✔ **Own Course Programme**
✔ **Venue for hire**
group self catering, several small spaces
⌣ 3 bedrooms with double beds, 1 bedroom with single bed. Self catering.
🚆 Nearest railway station is Builth Road or Llandrindod Wells; bus to Builth Wells or taxi.

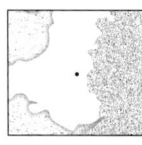

Dating from about 1870, Neuadd-Isaf Farmhouse is situated on a traditional working farm, one mile from the small market town of Builth Wells. Amidst unspoiled natural countryside it is ideal for small self-directed courses or retreats. It is an excellent base for walking, cycling or riding: we have stables and an all weather riding arena.

Natural therapies such as reflexology, aromatherapy and Indian head massage are available with nearby practitioners (by arrangement).

We look forward to welcoming you to a very special place where time has stood still.

Event Types
Self-directed retreats. Dowsing tuition available by arrangement.

Suitability
Adults and children 14 years and over.

The Old Rectory and Retreat Cottage

In the heart of the Pembrokeshire National Park in South Wales you find this extraordinary place. Here you can relax and heal your soul, body and spirit.

Two beautifully renovated C18th listed homes have their own charm and outstanding views over Newport Bay. From the slopes of Carn Ingli (angel mountain) the panoramic view extends along the famous coastline, beach, estuary, up to rocky crags and open moorlands.

Set in the acre of walled garden with separate private and communal areas, this historic site offers a thoughtfully designed venue for all interests. Here you can cook, dine, play, sunbathe, hide or pick our ripening fruits. Quietly situated 300m from the road it is surrounded by meadows.

Newport (Trefdraeth) is only a mile away. This ancient market town has a Norman castle, several excellent pubs and restaurants for all tastes and a wholefood store. Explore Newport's galleries, craft workshops, the golf course, the boat club and its one mile long beach.

A short walk takes you to the remarkable 186 mile long Pembrokeshire coast path, to dolmens, historic sites, wooded valleys and secluded coves. Nearby you find the Stonehenge Bluestone site in the Preseli mountains, an C11th Celtic cross, Neolithic tombs and stone circles.

Accommodation

Rectory has 6 bedrooms, Cottage has 3 bedrooms. Welsh Tourist Board 4 star accredited self-catering accommodation. Caterers available (from £10 per person per night). Large and smaller indoor spaces. One acre private walled garden. No smoking in buildings. Public transport available. Venue for hire for all ages, each property hired individually or together. Parties of 2-20 welcome.

Event Types

Venue suitable for self directed workshops and retreats. Family holidays. Reunions. Business workshops.

Subject Specialities

Previously used for meditation retreats, health and healing, storytelling, writing, martial arts, dance and musical workshops. Walking, cycling, rock climbing, astrology, Celtic culture, historic study, geological study and painting groups.

Gelli-Olau
Fishguard Road
Newport
Pembrokeshire
SA42 0UE

✆ 01239 820277
✆ 01239 820279
✉ info@go-wales.org

✔ **Retreat House**
✔ **Holiday Operator**
✔ **Venue for hire**
✎ 20 bedspaces (2 singles, 4 doubles, 1 twin, 2 family rooms, cots available)

Pen Rhiw

Tim Sime, Pen Rhiw, St Davids
Haverfordwest SA62 6PG
© 01437 721821
📞 01437 721821
📧 tim@penrhiw.co.uk

✔ **Retreat House**
✔ **Own Course Programme**
✔ **Venue for hire**

group full board (£43), self catering, large & small spaces

⚲ Up to 35 bedspaces in 21 rooms; almost all with washbasins. 4 doubles (1 en-suite), 7 singles, 7 twins, 1 family room. Full board, B&B, self-catering, central heating, no smoking in buildings, meditation room.

🍽 Special diets.

♿ Wheelchair access.

🚌 By train or coach to 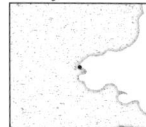 Haverfordwest, then taxi or Richards Bros bus to St Davids.

In the beautiful, powerful setting of the St Davids Peninsula in Britain's only coastal national park, Pen Rhiw is a fine, early Victorian rectory with a welcoming atmosphere. The main group room, a converted chapel with wonderful acoustics, is 52ft x 17ft. There is a living room with a log fire, over an acre of secluded grounds, a woodland terraced garden and seven acres of wildflower hay meadow which include rare species. It's a ten minute peaceful walk to the medieval Cathedral and Close and Whitesands Bay is a mile away. There is excellent, plentiful homecooked vegetarian food (organic garden). Open to all, families with children welcome.

Specialities include own course meditation workshops, retreats and guided walks (including sacred sites). Leader led spiritual groups, creative and performance arts, yoga, t'ai-chi, psychology, astrology, walkers.

Spirit Horse Foundation

A unique archaic place for personal change, community work, celebration and shamanic and spiritual practice in the wild. Founded in 1989 by Shivam O'Brien – Irish storyteller and ceremonialist and Erika Indra – Hungarian healer and counsellor. We emphasise a return to story, ritual and a re-building of sacred culture. This covers: ceremony, renewal, healing, counselling, ancient wisdom traditions, Celtic lore, meditation, sweat lodge, vigil, myth, poetry, being on the land, men's lodge, women's lodge, rites of passage, tribe, 'warrior decisions', 'authentic presence', taking responsibility, being real beyond therapy, risks, crazy for a while, dance, voice, music, pilgrimage, enlightenment intensives, reforestation, performance, work and celebration. Write for a current programme.

The venue: an enormous Celtic roundhouse for ceremonial meeting space (seats 200), huge Bedouin tent (main kitchen) and a magical village of tipis, yurts, and other traditional nomadic structures for sleeping, dreaming and being together. Secluded amongst 3000 acres of ancient forest, rockpools, waterfalls, rock face, meadow and moor. A superb, undisturbed setting for events close to nature and the elements. Rates unbeatable.

Eco-tourism features
Reforestation project. "Sacred Ecology" youth training programme. Rare wildlife/habitats. Low-impact, community-built mythical and sacred architecture. "Deep ecology" realised in traditional indigenous ritual space. Exemplary recycling. Compost toilets. No electricity.

Focus Ancient wisdom traditions worldwide; special emphasis on shamanic, Celtic, Buddhist, Sufi, Native American, Eastern, enlightenment traditions etc ... looking for the common thread.

19 Holmwood Gardens
Finchley
London N3 3NS
✆ 020 8346 3660
✉ indraerika@hotmail.com
✔ **Retreat House**
✔ **Own Course Programme**
✔ **Venue for hire**
group full board (from £20), group self catering (£7 to £15), large indoor space
⚲ Space/quarters for 10 to 200 in Celtic roundhouses, yurts, tipis, bedouin tents. Huge 38ft Celtic roundhouse for meetings, big ceremonies, dance etc. Viking mead hall-style kitchen seating 150 and able to cater for 300 plus.
🍽 Special diets.
♿ None (wildland).
🚍 We collect from Machynlleth Railway Station

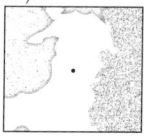

Trigonos

Plas Baladeulyn
Nantlle
Caernarfon
Gwynedd LL54 6BW
© 01286 882388
✆ 01286 882424
✉ info@trigonos.org
✔ **Retreat House**
✔ **Bed & Breakfast**
✔ **Own Course Programme**
✔ **Venue for hire**
group full board (£27 to £45), large & several small spaces
⌁ Standard occupancy 25 in mostly en-suite rooms, can be increased to 35. No smoking.
🍽 Delicious home-cooked meals largely, but not exclusively, vegetarian. Increasing organic and home grown produce. Special diets.
♿ Wheelchair access to public spaces, some bedrooms.
🚆 Bangor Station then Bus 5 to Nantlle or Caernarfon. Bus 80 from Caernarfon to Nantlle.

Trigonos lies within the Snowdonia National Park on the edge of the village of Nantlle. It is a site of spectacular natural beauty by the side of Llyn (Lake) Nantlle with a direct view across the lake and up the valley to Snowdon. The grounds include herb and vegetable gardens, fields, coppices, a stream and access to the lake itself. There is space for walking and quiet reflection, and easy access to the local countryside.

Venue Hire

Facilities include: gallery, suitable for yoga, tai chi, movement, performances;

large meeting room (up to 30 people); small meeting room, art studio/study

centre, lounge, library and 16 bedrooms.
We host groups running their own education and training programmes, retreats, holidays, art workshops, etc.

Course Programme

Our own courses include weaving and dyeing, art, social action and development, health & wellbeing and family-based events.

Bed & Breakfast

We welcome visitors of all ages, B&B or full-board (subject to availability).

Focus Interfaith

Other Places and Organisations

Ancient Healing Ways
Parc Bothy
Tan-y-bwlch, Maentwrog
Blaenau Ffestiniog
Gwynedd LL41 3AQ
Own Course Programme

Ardwyn
192 Gate Road
Penygroes, Llanelli
Carmarthenshire
SA14 7RW
Bed & Breakfast

Bryn Awel
Llangwm, Corwen
Denbighshire LL21 0RB
Bed & Breakfast

Caerwych Farm
Llandecwyn, Talsarnau
Gwynedd LL47 6YU
Venue for hire

Cefn Gribyn
Carmel
Llannerch-y-medd
Anglesey
LL71 7BU
Self catering

Coleg y Groes
Corwen
Denbighshire
LL21 0AU
Retreat House

Cryndir
Nantmel, Llandrindod Wells
Powys LD1 6EH
Venue for hire

Cwmllechwedd Fawr
Llanbister
Llandrindod Wells
Powys
LD1 6UH
Bed & Breakfast

Cwrt Y Cylchau
Llanfair Clydogau
Lampeter
Ceredigion
SA48 8LJ
✆ 01570 493526
Retreat House

Dyfed Permaculture Farm Trust
Bach y Gwyddel
Cwmpengraig
Drefach Felindre
Llandysul
SA44 5HX
✆ 01559 371424
🖰 jonogaunt@aol.com
Venue for Hire

Fraser Cottage
High Street
Bangor-on-Dee
Wrexham
Denbighshire
LL13 0AU
Bed & Breakfast

Other Places and Organisations

Graianfryn
Penisarwaun
Caernarfon
Gwynedd
LL55 3NH
Bed & Breakfast

Gwalia Farm
Cemmaes
Machynlleth
Powys
SY20 9PZ
Bed & Breakfast

**Hafod Cottage
& Art Studio**
Hafod
Maentwrog
Blaenau Ffestiniog
Gwynedd
LL41 3AQ
*Own Course
Programme*

Hendre Vegetarian B&B
Nantglyn
Denbigh
LL16 5PP
Bed & Breakfast

Hillscape
Blaen-y-Ddôl
Pontrhydygroes
Ystrad Meurig
Ceredigion
SY25 6DS
Holiday Operator

Llangasty Retreat House
Llangasty
Brecon
LD3 7PJ
✆ 01874 658250
Retreat House

Mandala Yoga Ashram
Pantypistyll
Llansadwrn
Llandeilo
Carmarthenshire
SA19 8NR
Own Course Programme

The Old Post Office
Llanigon
Hereford
HR3 5QA
Bed & Breakfast

The Old Rectory Hotel
Maentwrog
Blaenau Ffestiniog, Gwynedd
LL41 4HN
Bed & Breakfast

Outdoor Alternative
Cerrig yr Adar, Rhoscolyn
Holyhead, Anglesey
LL65 2NQ
Holiday Operator

**Panteidal Macrobiotic
Retreat**
Panteidal, Aberdyfi
Gwynedd LL35 0RG
Bed & Breakfast

Plas Madoc
60 Church Walks
Llandudno
Conwy
LL30 2HL
Bed & Breakfast

Rainbow Rose Retreats
Cefnllecoediog
Happy Valley
Pennal
Machynlleth
Powys
SY20 9LE
Retreat House

Snowdon Lodge
Lawrence House
Church Street
Tremadog
Portmadog
Gwynedd
LL49 9PS
Bed & Breakfast

Plas Taliaris
Llandeilo
Carmarthenshire
SA19 7NL
Venue for hire

**Taraloka Buddhist
Retreat Centre for Women**
Bettisfield
Whitchurch
Shropshire
SY13 2LD
℡ 0845 3304063
✉ admin@taraloka.org.uk
✿ http://www.taraloka.org.uk
Own Course Programme

Trericket Mill
Erwood
Builth Wells
Powys
LD2 3TQ
Bed & Breakfast

Ty'r Ysgol
Botwnnog
Pwllheli
Gwynedd
LL53 8PY
Bed & Breakfast

**Vajraloka Buddhist
Meditation Centre for Men**
Tyn-y-Ddol
Treddol
Corwen
Denbighshire
LL21 0EN
Retreat House

South West England

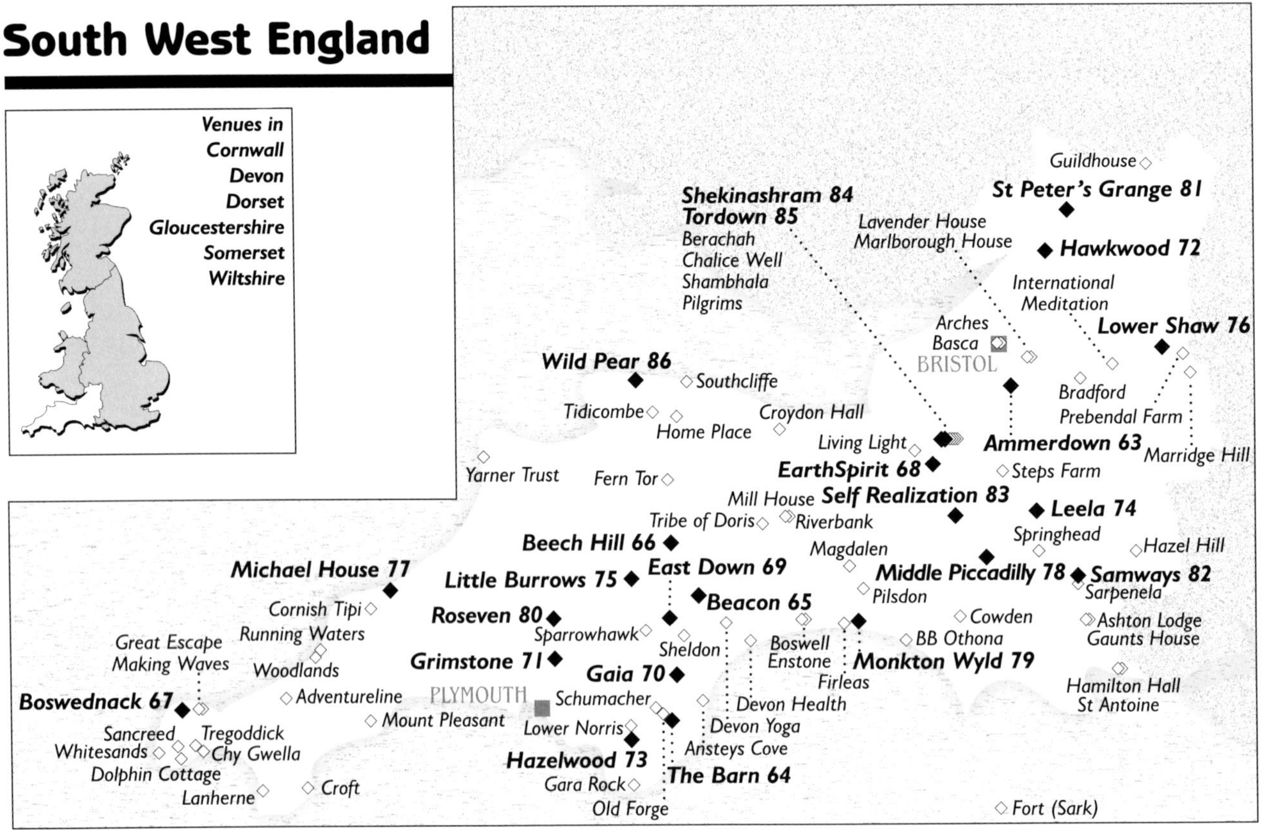

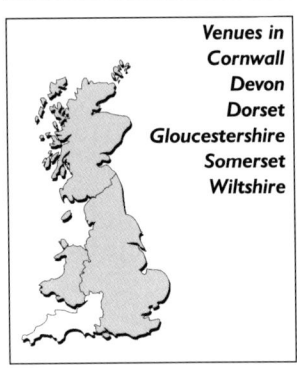

Venues in
Cornwall
Devon
Dorset
Gloucestershire
Somerset
Wiltshire

Guildhouse ◇

Shekinashram 84
Tordown 85
Berachah
Chalice Well
Shambhala
Pilgrims

Lavender House
Marlborough House

St Peter's Grange 81 ◆

◆ **Hawkwood 72**

International
Meditation

Lower Shaw 76 ◆

Arches
Basca ◇
◇
BRISTOL

Wild Pear 86
◆

◇ Southcliffe

Tidicombe ◇ ◇
Home Place

Croydon Hall

Living Light ◇

Bradford
Prebendal Farm

Ammerdown 63 Marridge Hill

Yarner Trust   Fern Tor ◇

EarthSpirit 68 ◆

◇ Steps Farm

Mill House **Self Realization 83**
Tribe of Doris ◇ Riverbank
Magdalen

◆ **Leela 74**
Springhead
◇ Hazel Hill

Beech Hill 66 ◆

East Down 69

◇ Pilsdon

Middle Piccadilly 78 ◆ **Samways 82**
Sarpenela

Michael House 77
◆

Cornish Tipi ◇
Running Waters
Woodlands

Little Burrows 75 ◆

Roseven 80 ◆
Sparrowhawk ◇

◆ **Beacon 65**
Sheldon

◇ Cowden
◇ BB Othona

Ashton Lodge
Gaunts House

Great Escape
Making Waves

Grimstone 71 ◆

Gaia 70 ◆

Boswell
Enstone

Monkton Wyld 79
Firleas

Boswednack 67 ◆

◇ Adventureline
PLYMOUTH
◇ Mount Pleasant

Schumacher ◇

◇ Devon Health

Hamilton Hall
St Antoine

Sancreed ◇ Tregoddick
Whitesands ◇ ◇ Chy Gwella
Dolphin Cottage
Lanherne ◇

◇ Croft

Lower Norris

Hazelwood 73
Gara Rock ◇

Devon Yoga
Aristeys Cove

The Barn 64

◇ Fort (Sark)

Old Forge ◇

⬧ http://www.ammerdown.org

Ammerdown is a retreat and conference centre located in beautiful, tranquil Somerset countryside. It has an excellent reputation for good food and a friendly atmosphere that sets the scene for an enjoyable experience.

Our programme includes spirituality retreats, interfaith, justice and peace, painting, holidays (literature, crafts, over 50s), prayer weekends, circle dance and day courses. There are our 'Quiet Spaces', including self-catering facilities, for those who wish to come and be away from the telephone and day to day pressures to walk, read, be listened to, or simply 'be'.

The Centre also provides excellent day or residential facilities for groups wishing to organise their own retreats, conferences and training, free from the many interruptions of the workplace.

As a holiday base there are many places of interest in the locality such as Wells, Bath, Glastonbury, Longleat and Cheddar.

Event Types
Guided group retreats, guided individual retreats, self directed retreats, own course pro-gramme, accredited courses.

Subject Specialities
Prayer, meditation, arts & crafts.

Suitability or Specialism
Adults, couples, families with children, women, men, young people 12 to 17, children under 12, older people.

Radstock
Bath
Somerset
BA3 5SW
✆ 01761 433709
🖷 01761 433094
✉ centre@ammerdown.org
✔ **Retreat House**
✔ **Bed & Breakfast**
✔ **Venue for hire**
group full board (£36 to £70), large indoor space, several small spaces
⌁ 58 bedspaces (31 singles, 7 twins, 1 double, 3 family rooms.)
🍽 Special diets.
♿ Wheelchair access.
🚌 Bath Spa station then regular bus services to Radstock, then taxi to Centre.

Focus
Christian and Interfaith

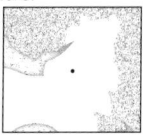

The Barn Retreat

Lower Sharpham Barton
Ashprington
Totnes
Devon
TQ9 7DX

✆ 01803 732661
📠 01803 732718
📧 barn@sharphamcollege.org

✔ **Retreat House**
✔ **Own Course Programme**
✔ **Venue for hire**

🛏 8 retreat rooms, one of which is a twin.
🍽 Exclusively vegetarian, special diets.
♿ None alas.
🚆 Train or coach to Totnes then 10 minute taxi ride.

Focus
Eclectic but Buddhist inspired.

Half-hidden behind giant beech trees on a hillside overlooking the river Dart, the Barn is one of the best-kept secrets in the English retreat circuit. Peace and quiet, fresh organic food, and the healing effect of meditation and reflection in a stunning natural location are some of the reasons people return again and again to take time out here from their usual routine. The Barn was established in 1986 to provide an environment where people could spend

anything from one week to six months practising meditation and learning to integrate it into their day-to-day lives. Supported by two residential managers, a changing group of up to eight retreatants share the gardening, cooking and household tasks, as well as three periods a day of silent group meditation.

Although Buddhist inspired, all faiths (or none) are equally welcome at the Barn. No meditation experience is needed, just willingness to participate.

Simple instructions are given if required, and teachers visit twice a week to answer questions. In term time there is the opportunity to attend evening talks at nearby Sharpham College.

During the afternoons and evenings, retreatants are encouraged to explore the 600-acre Sharpham estate of which the Barn property is a part, or pursue their own practice and creative activities. There is an optional yoga lesson once a week.

Block booking is possible in the quiet season, when, in consultation with the managers, a group may wish to create its own programme, whilst making full use of the Barn facilities.

Eco-tourism features
All organic cuisine, work period mainly in organic gardens.

The Beacon Centre

The Beacon Centre is situated within the attractive Devon hills. We offer a warm and welcoming venue for groups who are seeking a supportive, family atmosphere within which to work and be. Self-catering groups can enjoy uninterrupted use of the centre, including our well equipped and spacious kitchen.

Fine, varied and wholesome vegetarian food is our speciality for which we endeavour to use organic ingredients wherever possible.

The centre is cared for by a developing community of families and individuals who live at the farm. Our ethos is one of grounded, co-operative living, that seeks to restore harmony within ourselves, each other and the planet. The centre is open all year round, it is regularly used for courses in bodywork, professional training, therapeutic workshops, dance, movement and creative expression. We also work in association with a number of other organisations, providing day and residential space, for work with children and young people. Personal guided/unguided retreat space is also on offer during our quieter periods. For further information, please write, telephone or visit our website.

Ceri, Beacon Centre
Cutteridge Farm, Whitestone
Exeter, Devon EX4 2HE
☎ 01392 811203
✆ 01392 811203
✉ ceri@beacon-centre.com
✔ **Retreat House**
✔ **Bed & Breakfast**
✔ **Own Course Programme**
✔ **Venue for hire**
group full board (£35), B&B (£18) & self catering, large & small spaces
⚲ 24 bedspaces (6 twin, 2x3 bed, 1x4 bed, 1 double/twin). Camping (10), all ages welcomed, 1 large, 2 medium & several small workspaces.
🍽 Exclusively vegetarian/ organic (subject to availability), special diets,
🚌 3½ miles from both the train and coach station in Exeter.

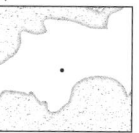

Beech Hill Community

http://web.onetel.net.uk/~beechhill/

Morchard Bishop
Crediton
Devon
EX17 6RF

© 01363 877228
✆ 01363 877587
✉ beechhill@ukonline.co.uk

✔ **Bed & Breakfast**
✔ **Venue for hire**
group full board (up to £32),
group self catering (up to
£16), large indoor space
⌐ 15 bedspaces (1 twin,
1 double, 2 dormitories.)
⦿ Special diets.
♿ Limited wheelchair access.
🚃 Nearest railway station,
Morchard Road, is 4 miles
away. Bus
from Exeter
3 times daily
to Morchard
Bishop
(1 mile).

Beech Hill is set in seven acres of grounds and gardens in a quiet, rural location midway between Dartmoor and Exmoor. Our course centre offers heated, small-dormitory accommodation; plus kitchen and large workspace suitable for t'ai chi, drumming, dance etc. The room is light and airy with a wood-burning stove, and opens on to a large lawn and gardens. A shady paddock provides good camping space, compost loo and outdoor shower. We offer superb wholefood catering using our own organic fruit and vegetables if available or, alternatively, courses can be self-catered. An outdoor swimming pool is available in summer months.

Event Types
Business retreats, accredited courses, working holidays.

Subject Specialities
Alternative lifestyles & technology, food & gardening, conservation work, rural skills, self expression, body & breathwork, health & healing, outdoor activities & sport, group process, ritual & shamanic.

Eco-tourism features
Communal living, organic growing, animals, compost toilet, reed bed water treatment, recycling, cob building, site for local compost scheme.

Boswednack Manor

Boswednack Manor comprises an old granite farmhouse with a cottage and group of barns around a grassy courtyard. The house itself is run as vegetarian guesthouse, and "Campion Cottage" is let on a self-catering basis. The barn spaces include a 36 x 16ft group work room and a separate meditation room plus barns for chickens, goats etc! There is a large organic vegetable garden, beautiful ornamental gardens with pond, outside chessboard and two meadows. The house and garden look down to the sea which is a few minutes' walk away and the Penwith Moors – rich in ancient sites like Men-an-Tol – are adjacent too. We offer B&B, wildlife walks, self-guided and facilitated retreats. Our programme includes movement and meditation, Yoga, Native American and Shamanistic weeks, and Buddhist retreats. We welcome enquiries from those who wish to bring their own group (of up to 16) to this special centre.

Event Types
Guided group and individual retreats, own course programme.

Subject Specialities
Meditation, body & breathwork, earth mysteries.

Suitability or Specialism
Adults, couples, families with children.

Eco-tourism features
Solar water heating and organic garden.

Dr E Gynn
Boswednack Manor
Zennor
St Ives
Cornwall
TR26 3DD
☎ 01736 794183

✔ **Retreat House**
✔ **Bed & Breakfast**
✔ **Own Course Programme**
✔ **Venue for hire**
group full board (£30 to £50), large indoor space
⌁ 10 bedspaces (1 single, 1 twin, 2 doubles, 1 family room.)
🍲 Exclusively vegetarian, special diets.
🚆 Train to Penzance or St Ives then bus 8, 8a or 15 will stop at our gate.

Focus
Buddhist/
Eco-spiritual

South West England/Cornwall

EarthSpirit

David Taylor
EarthSpirit
Dundon
Somerton
TA11 6PE

© 01458 272161
✆ 01458 273796
✉ earth.spirit1@virgin.net

✔ Retreat House
✔ Venue for hire

group full board, large indoor space, several small spaces
➲ 35 bedspaces (2 singles).
🍽 Exclusively vegetarian, special diets.
♿ Wheelchair access.
🚆 Castle Cary station 20 minutes by taxi (01963 351015)

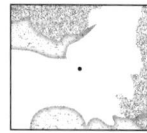

Focus
Eco-spirituality

Five miles from Glastonbury, EarthSpirit lies within the 'temenos' (sacred enclosure) of Avalon and is situated next to a wildlife reserve and a yew tree which is over 1,700 years old! EarthSpirit has a healing atmosphere but is not attached to any one tradition. We provide full facilities to groups of all kinds in our specially converted seventeenth century barn complex. The main hall is 52' long with oak timbers, reeds and stone walls; mediaeval, but with modern comforts such as under-floor heating and a large wood stove. A high roof and skylights create a light, airy atmosphere. Neighbouring B&B and camping can boost numbers. Seven acres of fields and gardens. Druidic tree circle, therapy room, sweat lodge and large hot tub all available. Group B&B is a possibility.

Event Types
Guided group retreats, accredited courses, teacher training, regeneration programmes etc.
Subject Specialities
Yoga, meditation, ritual & shamanic, health & healing, body & breath-work, inner process, counselling, group process etc.
Suitability or Specialism
Adults, couples.
Eco-tourism features
Caravans & camping, tipis.

http://www.eastdowncentre.co.uk

East Down Centre

Peaceful accommodation for small groups or workshops. No sharing with other groups. Self-catering or catered. Large group room. Sympathetically converted thatched barn set in beautiful country within the Dartmoor National Park.

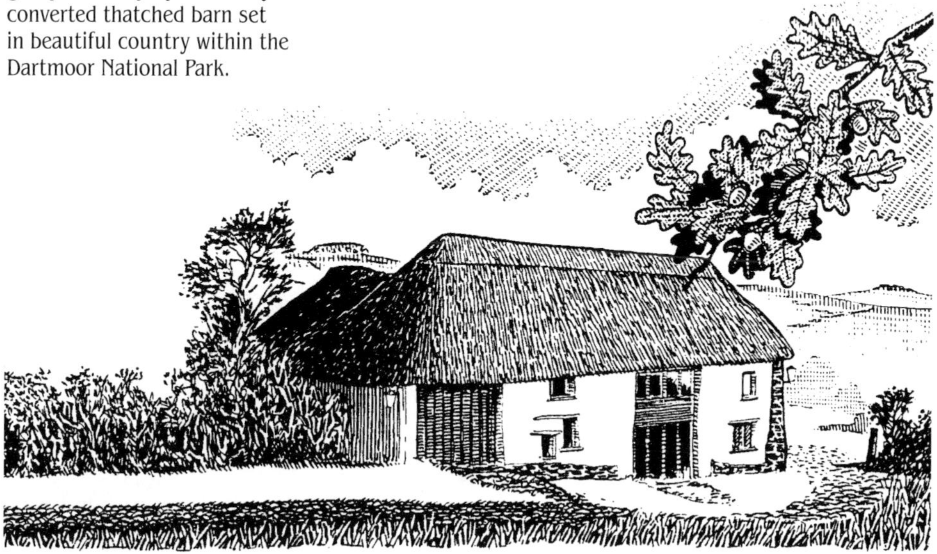

Leah Bond
East Down Centre
Dunsford
Exeter
Devon
EX6 7AL

✆ 01647 24041
01647 24041
leah@eastdowncentre.co.uk

✔ **Venue for hire**

group full board, group self catering, large indoor space

17 bedspaces (1 single, 1 twin, 1 x 4 beds, 2 x 5 beds).

Special diets catered for.

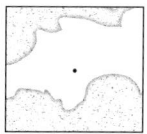

Gaia House

West Ogwell
Newton Abbot
Devon
TQ12 6EN

© 01626 333613
01626 352650

generalenquiries@gaiahouse.co.uk
✔ **Retreat House**
✔ **Own Course Programme**
80 bedspaces.
Vegetarian. Special diets catered for.
Ground floor rooms, with full accessibility to rest of house.
By train or coach to Newton Abbot. Taxi or walk to Gaia House (approx 2 miles).

Focus
Buddhist/
Vipassana

Gaia House is set in a former convent in the stunning countryside of South Devon and offers a sanctuary of contemplative calm open to all. Gaia House is a non-affiliated retreat centre offering guidance in different meditative disciplines from the Buddhist tradition. Our retreats are designed for both experienced meditators and beginners, of any faith or none, who seek to cultivate a path of wisdom and compassion. All retreats are held in silence with the exception of the Family and Friends retreat.

We offer a full programme of group retreats throughout the year varying in length from a weekend to nine days led by internationally renowned teachers. Retreats mainly focus on the practice of Insight (vipassana), Loving Kindness (metta) and Zen meditation.

Each group retreat day includes a full schedule of sitting and walking meditation, group or individual interviews, a talk and meditation instructions. A separate wing of the house provides facilities for people wishing to undertake a personal retreat in a supportive environment with regular guidance from teachers. We also offer five work retreat places at no charge in exchange for work towards the running of Gaia House.

Grimstone Manor is a residential venue on the edge of Dartmoor, 9 miles north of Plymouth and 4 miles south of Tavistock. It is a comfortable house with full central heating, an indoor swimming pool, jacuzzi and sauna.

Set in over 20 acres of grounds, the centre is run by a community helped by local people and occasional volunteers.

Food is mainly vegetarian and drinks and snacks are available in the dining room 24 hours a day. Where possible we try to use organic and fairtrade products; we also stock a good range of organic vegetarian wine and beers.

The Manor is open to courses all year; it is used regularly for courses in yoga, dance, healing, psychotherapy, massage and developmental training of numerous kinds, as well as a small number of holiday and working breaks.

Event Types
Guided group retreats, own course programme.

Subject Specialities
Inner process, group process, bodywork, ritual & shamanic, counselling, health & healing, alternative lifestyles & technology, self expression, conservation work, food & gardening, meditation.

Suitability or Specialism
Adults(++), couples(+), families with children(+), women, men, older people.

Jordan Lane, Horrabridge
Yelverton, Devon PL20 7QY
© 01822 854358

enquiries@grimstonemanor.co.uk
✔ **Own Course Programme**
✔ **Venue for hire**
group full board (£44 to £48), large indoor space, several small spaces
↝ 40 bedspaces including singles, doubles and shared rooms.
🍽 Special diets.
♿ Wheelchair access.
🚌 Trains and coaches to Plymouth (National Rail: 0845 7484950; National Express Coaches: 0870 5808080). Local bus (0870 6082608) or Taxifast (01752 222222) to Horrabridge.

Focus
Eco-spiritual

Hawkwood

Richard Brinton
Hawkwood
Painswick Old Road,
Stroud
Gloucestershire GL6 7QW
© 01453 759034
℡ 01453 764607
info@hawkwoodcollege.co.uk

✔ **Retreat House**
✔ **Bed & Breakfast**
✔ **Own Course Programme**
✔ **Venue for hire**
group full board, large indoor space, several small spaces
↝ 51 bedspaces (14 singles, 17 twins.)
🍽 Special diets.
♿ Wheelchair access.
🚘 Energetic 25 minute walk or taxi from Stroud railway station.

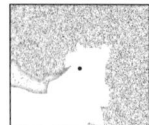

Focus
Broadly Anthroposophical

A beautiful and peaceful setting. Situated at the head of a small Cotswold valley with panoramic views down to the Severn Vale. Comfortable accommodation. Well stocked library with log fire, large sitting room with piano. Extensive grounds host a wealth of flora and fauna, and a spring which provides drinking water. Walled organic

garden supplies many ingredients for delicious meals. Within an Area of Outstanding Natural Beauty (AONB) with many miles of footpaths, and many lovely villages. Slad Valley (birthplace of author Laurie Lee), and Painswick with its famous churchyard are both nearby. Wide range of short courses including music, arts and crafts, and personal and spiritual development. While the spiritual impulse is the work of Rudolf Steiner, part of Hawkwood's mission is to bring anthroposophy into a fruitful interaction with other artistic and spiritual streams. This is reflected in the broad range of courses on offer.

Event Types
Guided group retreats, self directed retreats, business retreats, own course programme.

Subject specialities
Music, arts & crafts, health & healing, creative expression, meditation, couples work, death & dying, yoga, Celtic studies, earth mysteries, spirituality.

Suitability or Specialism
Adults and couples of all ages.

Hazelwood House

Hazelwood, in the heart of the South Devonshire countryside, is a place of extraordinary peace and beauty. There are 67 acres of woodland, meadows, riverbank and orchards which are ideal for walking, painting or simply relaxing. Hazelwood is perfect for rest and reflection. Hazelwood House itself, which is early Victorian, is open 365 days a year. We offer accommodation and delicious food, mainly locally produced organic meat and vegetables freshly cooked for non-vegetarians and vegetarians alike. Guests may enjoy the comfort of log fires during the winter or relax on the veranda in summer. Four holiday cottages spread over the estate offer the possibility of self-catering accommodation. Concerts, cultural events and courses take place at Hazelwood throughout the year. We have a varied programme and would be pleased to put you on our mailing list. We have a licence to host civil weddings.

Event Types
Guided group retreats, self directed retreats, business retreats, own course programme.

Subject Specialities
Alternative lifestyles & technology, food & gardening, conservation work, health & healing, earth mysteries.

Jane Bowman
Hazelwood House
Loddiswell
Kingsbridge
Devon
TQ7 4EB
✆ 01548 821232
📠 01548 821318
✔ **Retreat House**
✔ **Bed & Breakfast**
✔ **Own Course Programme**
✔ **Venue for hire**
group full board (£40 to £70), group self catering, large indoor space
🛏 60 bedspaces (23 singles, 13 twins, 12 doubles, 3 family rooms.)
🍽 Special diets.
♿ Wheelchair access.
🚉 Totnes Station then Ray's Taxi Service (01803) 664567

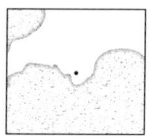

The Leela Centre

Veeren
Thorn Grove House
Common Mead Lane
Gillingham
Dorset
SP8 4RE

✆ 01747 821221
📠 01747 826386
📧 info@osholeela.co.uk

✔ Venue for hire
group full board (£33 to £50), large indoor space, several small spaces

⤳ 72 bedspaces (13 doubles, 10 dormitories.)

🍽 Exclusively vegetarian, special diets.

♿ Wheelchair access to ground floor.

🚌 National Express 1x daily London. London-Exeter mainline train to Gillingham (Dorset).

Focus Eastern

After four years near Wimborne, The Leela Centre, Britain's most vibrant and friendly centre moved to Gillingham (Dorset) in April 2000. It's a beautiful big house in wonderful north Dorset countryside. Leela also has its own registered caravan and camping park next door with excellent facilities. Leela is increasingly visited by people who want to relax, make friends and enjoy the atmosphere of celebration and naturalness. When featured on the BBC documentary 'Heaven and Earth' Toyah Wilcox was rapturously enthusiastic about the Leela Centre – "It's really fantastic. It's the first time I've opened up in 41 years". Situated between Stonehenge and Glastonbury, Leela's most popular programme is the monthly Super Special weekend, an introduction to the Leela community. On this low cost weekend, participants join the community in work, meditation, partying and hanging out. You are very welcome to come along and connect with our expanding network of life positive friends.

Event Types
Guided group retreats, own course programme, working holidays.

Subject Specialities
Self expression, group process, meditation, body & breathwork, health & healing, inner process, counselling.

Suitability or Specialism
Adults, couples, families with children, older people.

Eco-tourism features
Caravan and camping park. Nature walk in 12 acres of new trees.

Little Burrows Holiday & Retreat Centre

Little Burrows is situated in a peaceful and beautiful corner of Dartmoor, with nearby streams, rock pools, woodland walks and vast expanses of moorland with stone circles, rugged tors, singing skylarks and grazing ponies.

Kristin and Richard offer a quiet, beautiful, secluded place for retreats and creativity or an alternative holiday among like minded people. Accommodation consists of self-catering wooden cabins, caravan and rooms in house. All meals are all organic and vegetarian. Vegan, wheat free and other diets can be catered for.

Kristin and Richard are artists who also enjoy making music and offer a fully equipped recording studio with a grand piano for those wanting to make a CD and an art studio

for those wanting to combine their holiday with something more creative. There is a mature garden with ponds and a waterfall, organic vegetable garden and wood burning sauna.

A place to just 'BE' and reconnect to one's innermost nature.

Eco-tourism features
All food is organic, fresh herbs from the garden, home cooking. All cleaning products green, gardening organic, low energy lighting and heating.

Focus All embracing

Shilstone Lane, Throwleigh Okehampton, Devon EX20 2HX
✆ 01647 231305
✉ kristin@
organicaccommodation.com
✔ **Retreat House**
✔ **Bed & Breakfast**
✔ **Holiday Operator**
✔ **Own Course Programme**
✔ **Venue for hire**
group full board (£40 to £46), group self catering (£15 to £22), large small spaces
🛏 10 beds (4 singles, 4 twins, 4 doubles, 2 family rooms, 3 cabins and 1 caravan.)
🍴 Excl vegtrian, special diets.
♿ Wheelchair access.
🚆 Train or bus to Exeter then bus X9 or X10 to Whiddon Down followed by 2 mile walk. We can pick you up from Exeter or Whiddon Down.

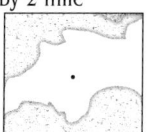

Lower Shaw Farm

 http://www.lowershawfarm.co.uk

Old Shaw Lane
Shaw, Swindon
Wiltshire
SN5 5PJ
© 01793 771080
📠 01793 771080
📧
enquiries@lowershawfarm.co.uk
✔ **Bed & Breakfast**
✔ **Own Course Programme**
✔ **Venue for hire**
group full board (£30), several small spaces
🛏 30 bedspaces (7 singles, 4 doubles, 7 family rooms, 4 dormitories.)
🍽 Exclusively vegetarian, special diets.
♿ Wheelchair access to most of farm.
🚃 Train to Swindon then

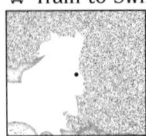

short local bus ride.

Focus
Humanist

Lower Shaw Farm offers weekend breaks, working and learning holidays, as well as opportunities for volunteering. Typically, our programme includes craft courses such as willow basket and felt making, organic gardening and wholefood cookery, yoga, walking with nature, and African drumming. There is an annual literature festival, a juggling and circus skills holiday, a singing and music weekend, and seasonal Family Activity Holidays. The farm is also available for hire by groups and conference organisers.

Once a dairy farm deep in rural North Wiltshire, Lower Shaw Farm now has another life: as a three-acre oasis in an area of 1980s development. The farm has kept a character and atmosphere of its own, with organic gardens, living willow structures, ponds, poultry, sheep, a campfire circle, and play spaces for both children and adults. Lower Shaw is run by a family of five with a network of helpers, local, national, and international.

The outbuildings have been converted into meeting rooms, workshops, and accommodation, much of which is accessible to people with disabilities – please ask for details. The accommodation is basic, but homely. There is a visitors' kitchen for drinks and snacks, and small and large group rooms. The organic vegetarian meals are prepared with mostly homegrown and locally produced ingredients. Not far away is Avebury and the Ridgeway.

Programme of courses, and hire/B&B charges, available on request. We welcome telephone enquiries. Life is for learning at Lower Shaw Farm!

Michael House

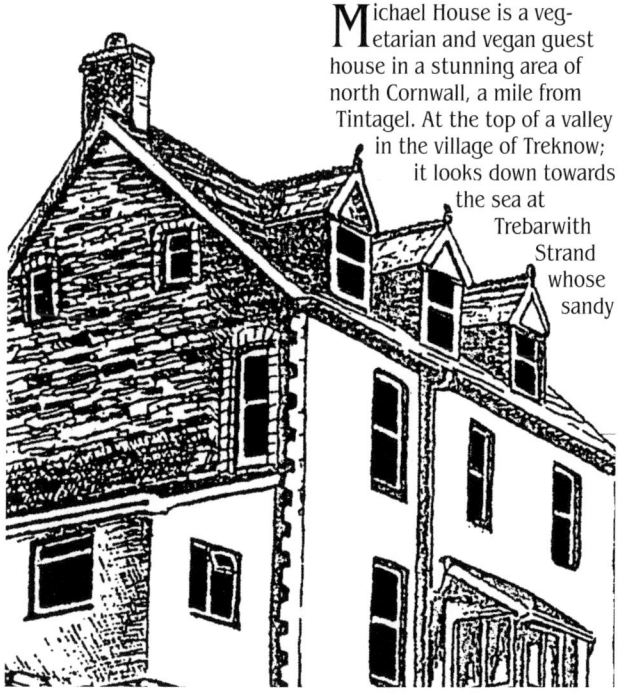

Michael House is a vegetarian and vegan guest house in a stunning area of north Cornwall, a mile from Tintagel. At the top of a valley in the village of Treknow; it looks down towards the sea at Trebarwith Strand whose sandy beach has a dramatic cliff backdrop.

We offer delicious vegetarian or vegan evening meals and have a full licence. We grow some of our vegetables and use a range of fairly traded, or local or organic produce wherever possible. The house is non-smoking.

There are three double en-suite rooms, one of which can be a twin room, and another can be a family room. They all enjoy views towards the sea and over countryside and have a restful atmosphere. The sitting room and gardens are available for the use of guests.

Michael House is open all year, please check the web site for autumn and spring special offers, and we are open over the Christmas period. Please do contact us for any further information you may require.

Vanessa Lackford
Michael House
Trelake Lane
Treknow
Tintagel
Cornwall
PL34 0EW

© 01840 770592
info@michael-house.co.uk

✔ **Bed & Breakfast**
✔ **Venue for hire**

6 bedspaces (1 twin, 2 doubles)
Vegetarian and vegan. Special diets catered for.

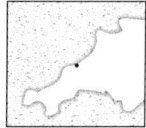

Middle Piccadilly Healing Centre

Dominic Harvey
Middle Piccadilly
Holwell
Sherborne
Dorset
DT9 5LW

℡ 01963 23468
✆ 01963 23764
✆ info@middlepiccadilly.com

✔ **Retreat House**
✔ **Bed & Breakfast**
✔ **Own Course Programme**
✔ **Venue for hire**

↘ 9 bedspaces (3 singles, 1 twin, 2 doubles.)
🍽 Exclusively vegetarian.
🚂 Sherborne Station then taxi (with Beaver Cabs 01935 816620) to Middle Piccadilly

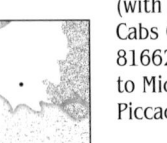

Experience the magic of Middle Piccadilly – The Alternative Health Farm. Middle Piccadilly is a fully residential Natural Healing Centre established in September 1986; the building itself is a 17th Century thatched country house and stable wing lovingly converted and attractively furnished to provide accommodation for up to 9 residents. The surrounding Dorset countryside is especially beautiful: the peaceful and tranquil atmosphere is almost tangible at the centre. It is first and foremost a place of healing: the purpose of the centre is to provide a welcoming and informal atmosphere, where guests feel totally at home. The centre offers a residential programme of Wholistic Health Intensives, which include an extensive range of alternative therapies and specialist baths in our aquaspa that help to relieve our guests of all the pressures and stresses of modern life, and promote the process of self healing.

Event Types
Guided individual retreats, self directed retreats, business retreats, own courses.

Subject Specialities
Health & healing, alternative medicine.

Suitability or Specialism
Adults(+), couples(+), women(+), men(+), older people(+).

Monkton Wyld Court

Our Centre for Holistic Education offers an exciting and varied programme of residential courses, ranging from shamanism and Tibetan healing exercises to yoga and singing workshops; plus the ever-popular Family Weeks throughout the year. We also offer B&B accommodation, whenever possible.

The centre is run by a full time community of 10-16 adults plus their children, with help from visiting volunteers. The main house is a neo-gothic Victorian rectory which sleeps up to 35 guests. It is set alongside a few outbuildings and is located in a beautiful Dorset valley, three miles from the sea at Lyme Regis. The 11 acre estate comprises a small dairy and chicken farm, a walled organic vegetable garden, terraced lawns, children's play area, woods and a stream. Other spaces available to guests include two large group rooms, a sitting room with piano, library, meditation hut, healing room, craft shop, pottery and arts facilities. We invite you to discover, escape, relax and learn something new.

Event Types
Group programme and venue courses, educational holidays.

Subject Specialities
Family, yoga, meditation, ritual & shamanic, health & healing, body & breathwork, singing, inner process, conservation work, arts & crafts, alternative lifestyles & technology.

Suitability or Specialism
Adults, families with children.

Charmouth
Bridport
Dorset
DT6 6DQ
✆ 01297 560342
📠 01297 560395

monktonwyldcourt@btinternet.com
✔ **Bed & Breakfast**
✔ **Own Course Programme**
✔ **Venue for hire**
group full board (£37 to £42), large and small spaces
↪ 35 bedspaces (3 twins, 1 double, 8 dormitories)
🍽 99% organic, exclusively vegetarian, special diets.
♿ Some wheelchair access to ground floor of main house.
🚂 Axminster railway station 4 miles away.
Taxi, or Bus 31 to Hunters Lodge followed by 1 mile walk.

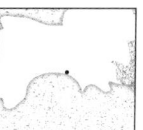

Roseven Centre

http://www.roseven.co.uk

Woodmanswell
North Brentor
Tavistock
Devon
PL19 0NE

© 01822 820416
℡ 01822 820416
✆ info@roseven.co.uk
✔ **Retreat House**
✔ **Venue for hire**
group self catering (£15 to £20), large indoor space
⇲ 23 bedspaces (1 single, 4 twins, 3 double, 6 others)
& No wheelchair access.
🚃 Train to Exeter or Plymouth then buses to Tavistock.
Focus All embracing

D at Rosa Mel Apibus – The Rose gives honey to the Bees
Originally a Rosicrucian emblem, we admit, but it seems very apt to describe the Roseven Centre mission. Situated at the Old Farmstead of Woodmanswell in West Devon, the Roseven centre nestled on the side of the wooded Lyd valley, on the Western slopes of Dartmoor. Totally secluded at the end of a half mile private track, it offers a chance to disengage from the world of the 21st Century and recharge, just as the bees recharge their honey stocks for winter.
Two springs emerge in the pond garden where a natural energetic tranquillity creates a perfect atmosphere for meditation and at-one-ness.
Brentor, crowned by the tiny church of St Michael of the Rock, a close cousin of Glastonbury Tor but without the crowds, rises up a mile and a half away. Its complementary partner, the beautiful Lydford gorge, with a hundred and fifty foot White Lady Waterfall and scary Devil's Cauldron is also within one mile of the Centre. We invite you to come and look around (by appointment) and like the Bees, receive Honey from the Sevenfold Petalled Rose.
We host retreats and workshops of all kinds and are also available for holidays.

A 16th century house of prayer in 500 acres of Cotswold parkland with views across the Severn valley towards the Malvern Hills. It is an extension of the Abbey Guest Wing (men only) but for everyone. Guests are invited to join the Community in the Abbey Church for Services (five a day).

The Grange is also open to any group for residential or day retreats. Accommodation is comfortable though simple, with hot and cold water in all rooms and separate shower/bathrooms. There are four spacious sitting rooms, a chapel, a dining room seating 50 and simple home cooking with attention to any special dietary needs. No smoking in the building. Except for four led Days of Recollection each year, groups are normally hosted here and bring their own retreat director with them. Exceptionally, however, Father Abbot may be contacted to request a leader from the Community if a group is unable to supply its own.

Events

Led Days (and or weekends) of Recollection, self-directed retreats, hosting of group retreats with their own programme. Suitable for adults, couples, families with children and older people.

Focus Christian/Catholic

Prinknash Abbey, Cranham
Gloucester GL4 8EX
✆ 01452 813592
📠 01452 814187
✉ spgprinknash@freeuk.com
✔ **Retreat House**
✔ **Bed & Breakfast**
✔ **Venue for hire**
group full board (£35 to £37), large & small spaces
⌁ 33 beds (3 singles, 4 doubles with additional single beds, 2 twins, 4 family rooms.)
🍽 Special diets.
♿ Portable ramps inside, over 2 flights of 2 steps each. Exterior access/exit one step. Ground floor accommodation.
🚌 Stroud-Cheltenham bus departs hourly in both directions. Alight at Cranham Corner, cross to half-timbered lodge, down hill inside estate.

Samways Farm

Claire Morris
Samways
Alvediston
Salisbury
Wiltshire
SP5 5LQ

℡ 01722 780286
✆ claire@samwaysfarm.co.uk

✔ **Bed & Breakfast**
✔ **Own Course Programme**
✔ **Venue for hire**
group full board, group self catering, large indoor space, several small spaces
⤳ 16 bedspaces (3 twins, 2 self-catering cottages, 1 shepherd's hut)
🍽 Exclusively vegetarian, special diets.
🚍 Train to Tisbury (5 miles)

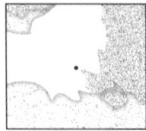 or Salisbury (13 miles) then taxi or infrequent bus.

🕸 http://www.samwaysfarm.co.uk

Samways Farm is a beautiful complex of listed buildings situated in the Cranborne Chase designated Area of Outstanding Natural Beauty. The farm has been used as a location in several period films including Thomas Hardy's "The Woodlanders".

The farmhouse has three lovely en-suite twin rooms for B&B and there are also two comfortable self-catering cottages, each sleeping four, and a Shepherd's Hut with a double bed. It is a wonderful place for walking, cycling, riding, bird watching or just taking it easy and there are plenty of interesting sites to explore locally – Salisbury, Bath, Stonehenge, Avebury, the stunning World Heritage Dorset coastline. Within the farm courtyard is a converted eighteenth century stone barn with wooden floor (19'6" x 56'6") that can be used for celebrations and workshops and there are two good-sized rooms in the house (17'6" x 20' with open fireplace and 15'6" x 22'6" with wood burner). We run our own yoga, walking and riding holidays but welcome enquires from those who wish to hire the facilities for their own group or workshop.

Self Realization Meditation Healing Centre

The Centre is a charitable trust founded by Mata Yoganandaji to help people – of all beliefs and none – find peace and fulfilment. Run by a spiritual family of teachers, healers and counsellors, providing courses, individual appointments, retreats and nurturing breaks, it is a spiritual home in every sense – with unconditional love as the watchword. Pure Meditation courses are held regularly and all are welcome to join the morning and evening meditations. There are three acres of beautiful gardens, log fires in winter, a library and therapy pool. Home-cooked vegetarian meals – special diets catered for. Please ask for a colour brochure and full course programme, including Pure Meditation courses, Professional Healer and Counsellor Training, Self Development, Hatha and Aqua Yoga and Teacher Training courses.

Event Types
Guided group retreats, guided individual retreats, self directed retreats, business retreats, own course programme, accredited courses, teacher training, regeneration programmes.

Subject Specialities
Meditation, body & breathwork, counselling, group & inner process, health & healing, prayer, self expression, Transformation Hatha Yoga.

Eco-tourism features
Garden retreat chalet accommodation with ecological Bio-Let toilet. Organic homegrown vegetables and salad (where possible).

Laurel Lane
Queen Camel
Yeovil
Somerset
BA22 7NU

℅ 01935 850266
℡ 01935 850234
🖅 info@selfrealizationcentres.org
✔ **Retreat House**
✔ **Own Course Programme**
↴ 31 bedspaces (7 twins, 2 family rooms.)
♿ Disabled bedroom. New teaching room has disabled access.
🚗 Approximately 5 miles from both Castle Cary and Sherborne railway stations. Taxis available and we are sometimes able to collect guests.

Focus
All welcome

Shekinashram

Dod Lane
Glastonbury
BA6 8BZ
✆ 01458 832300
✉ info@shekinashram.org
✔ **Bed & Breakfast**
✔ **Retreat House**
✔ **Own Course Programme**
↝ Maximum 10 bed spaces.
B&B (£16 sharing - £25 single - £45 twin or double - £60 triple) or full board. No smoking or alcohol in house or garden. 32 x 16 foot group room for hire. Sauna & office facilities.
🍽 Exclusively vegan raw food.
🚌 Local bus from Bath or Bristol to Glastonbury or train to Castle Cary, then 20 minute taxi journey. 5 minutes walk from Glastonbury town centre.

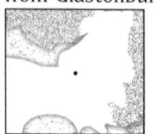

Focus Eco-Spiritual/Non-dualistic

Shekinashram is a newly formed community and dedicated sacred space, situated at the base of Chalice Hill, on a pilgrimage route to Glastonbury Tor. There are currently five permanent residents at the ashram. We are open all year round and welcome guests to join us in this inspirational, transformative space. Essentially the vision of the Shekinashram is to express a way of life that is both conscious and selfless, and which deeply honours the One in all its miraculous forms. We live according to a set of holistic principles, and maintain the ashram in a spacious way that is intentionally free from unnecessary distractions. This environment is naturally conducive to the development of spiritual practise and the cultivation of internal disciplines.

It is intended that this way of life genuinely reflects freedom of Being. We promote an abundant and sustainable lifestyle, enjoy an organic vegan raw food diet, meditate, practice yoga and sing devotional songs together. A commitment to living Self-Realisation and a willingness to enter into profound relationship underpins our being together.

We have a group room for hire, and are able to accommodate

up to 10 guests on residential workshops. We also have bed and breakfast accommodation available for short and longer term paying guests, and a growing programme of events, workshops, and retreats. We also offer morning meditation, one to one therapeutic treatments, raw food lunches, fresh juices, sauna and office facilities.

Event Types
Healing breaks, cleansing retreats, weekend courses, guided group & self directed retreats, own course programme, evening groups, daily meditation, devotional singing.

Subject Specialities
Spiritual development, meditation, raw food nutrition, health and healing, group and inner process.

S ituated on the southern slopes of the Tor overlooking the Vale of Avalon. Television, basin, tea and coffee making facilities in all rooms, with many en suite. Vegetarian, no smoking, own car park, garden, patio with glorious views, waterfall and pond. Two Reiki Masters in residence. Also available: Ear Candeling; Higher Self Communication Sessions; Hydrotherapy pool; Multidimensional Cellular healing; Reset and Whole Health Body Scans; Massage can be arranged. Family run with a welcoming, friendly, peaceful and spiritual atmosphere. Varied accommodation. Choose from our Citrene, Clear Quartz, Amethyst, Malachite Lapis and Rose Quartz rooms or our Angelic Opal suites. Library containing some of the oldest and newest spiritual/ healing books. A place to be peaceful, refind yourself, relax and enjoy. English Tourist Board: 4 diamonds.

Event Types
Guided group retreats, guided individual retreats, self directed retreats, own course programme, teacher training.

Subject Specialities
Health & healing, inner process.

Suitability or Specialism
Adults.

Sherhadasha and Michael Penn
Tordown
5 Ashwell Lane
Glastonbury
Somerset
BA6 8BG

✆ 01458 832287
📠 01458 831100
📧 michael@tordown.com

✔ **Retreat House**
✔ **Bed & Breakfast**
✔ **Own Course Programme**
↝ 14 bedspaces (2 singles, 2 twins, 1 double, 2 family rooms.)
🍽 Exclusively vegetarian.
🚌 Train to Castle Cary then 20 minute taxi ride. Buses from Bath, Bristol or London.

Wild Pear Centre

King Street
Combe Martin
Devon
EX34 0AG

✆ 020 8341 7226
✆ 020 8341 7226
✉ wildpearinfo@
primalintegration.com
✔ **Retreat House**
✔ **Venue for hire**
*group full board (£30 to £35),
group self catering (£15 to
£18), large indoor space, several small spaces*
➭ 25 bedspaces (3 twins,
2 doubles, 5 dormitories.)
🍽 Special diets.
🚆 Train to Barnstaple then
bus or taxi to Combe Martin,
alternatively
coach to
Ilfracombe
then bus or
taxi

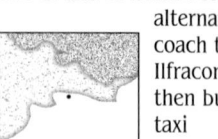

A centre for personal growth work located in a seaside village on the edge of Exmoor National Park and close to spectacular coastal scenery and secluded beaches. With a large group room and communal hall, generously equipped with cushions, work mattresses and a piano, the centre is a suitable workshop venue for a variety of group activities such as yoga, meditation, growth groups, bodywork, movement and dance. Available for hire for residential or non-residential use (full board or self-catered) at reasonable rates, the centre also welcomes individual or group retreats or groups on holiday.

Event Types
Guided group retreats, self directed retreats.

Subject Specialities
Body & breathwork, counselling, earth mysteries, group process, health & healing, inner process, meditation, ritual and shamanic, self expression.

Suitability or Specialism
Adults.

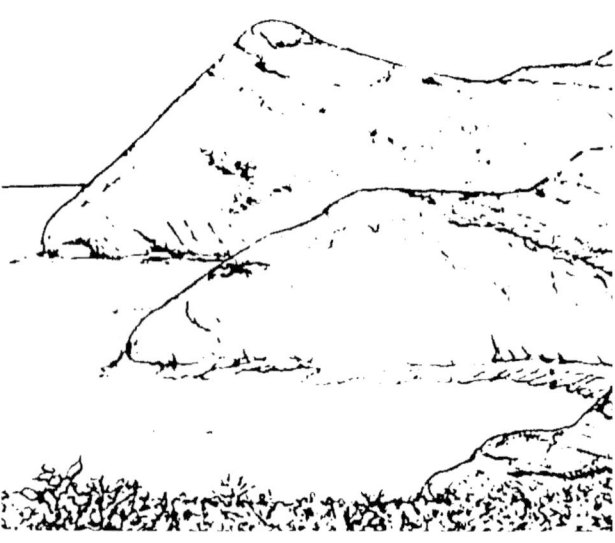

Other Places and Organisations

Adventureline
North Trefula Farm, Redruth
Cornwall TR16 5ET
Holiday Operator

Ansteys Cove Hotel
327 Babbacombe Rd, Torquay
Devon TQ1 3TB
Bed & Breakfast

Arches Hotel
32 Cotham Brow, Cotham
Bristol BS6 6AE
Bed & Breakfast

Ashton Lodge
Stanbridge, Wimborne
Dorset BH21 4JQ
Venue for hire

Basca House
19 Broadway Road, Bishopston
Bristol BS7 8ES
Bed & Breakfast

**Berachah Colour
Healing Centre**
Well House Lane, Glastonbury
Somerset BA6 8BJ
Bed & Breakfast

Boswell Farm
Sidford, Sidmouth, Devon
EX10 0PP
Venue for hire

Bradford Old Windmill
4 Masons Lane
Bradford-on-Avon, Wiltshire
BA15 1QN
Bed & Breakfast

Burton Bradstock Othona
Coast Road, Burton Bradstock
Bridport, Dorset DT6 4RN
Retreat House

Chalice Well Trust
Chilkwell Street, Glastonbury
Somerset BA6 8DD
Retreat House

Chy Gwella
53 Morrab Road, Penzance
Cornwall, TR18 4EX
Bed & Breakfast

Cornish Tipi Holidays
Tregeare, Pendoggett, St Kew
Bodmin, Cornwall PL30 3LW
info@cornish-tipi-
holidays.co.uk
01208 880781
Retreats

Cowden House
Frys Lane, Godmanstone
Dorchester, Dorset
DT2 7AG
Bed & Breakfast

The Croft
North Corner, Coverack
Helston, Cornwall TR12 6TF
Bed & Breakfast

Croydon Hall
Rodhuish
Minehead
Somerset
TA24 6QT
Venue for hire

Devon Health Spa
30 West Hill
Budleigh Salterton, Devon
EX9 6BU
Retreat House

Other Places and Organisations

Devon School of Yoga
1 Barton Cottages
Sowton Village, Exeter
Devon EX5 2AF
Own Course Programme

Dolphin Cottage
Women's B&B
Newtown, St Buryan
Penzance, Cornwall TR19 6BQ
Bed & Breakfast

Enstone Guesthouse
Lennox Avenue, Sidmouth
Devon EX10 8TX
Bed & Breakfast

Fern Tor Vegetarian and
Vegan Guest House
Meshaw, South Molton
Devon
EX36 4NA
Bed & Breakfast

Firleas
8 Colway Close, Lyme Regis
Dorset DT7 3BE
Bed & Breakfast

Le Fort
Sark, Guernsey
Channel Islands GY9 0SF
Own Course Programme

Gara Rock
East Portlemouth, Salcombe
Devon TQ8 8PH
Bed & Breakfast

Gaunts House
Wimborne, Dorset BH21 4JQ
Own Course Programme

The Great Escape
16 Parc Avenue, St Ives
Cornwall TR26 2DN
Bed & Breakfast

The Guildhouse
Stanton, Broadway
WR12 7NE
Venue for hire

Hamilton Hall
1 Carysfort Road, Boscombe
Bournemouth, Dorset BH1 4EJ
Own Course Programme

Hazel Hill Woodland
Retreat Centre
c/o Garden Lodge
Winchester Rd, Kings Somborne
Stockbridge SO20 6NY
Own Course Programme

Home Place
Home Place Farm
Challacombe, Barnstaple
Devon EX31 4TS
Bed & Breakfast

International
Meditation Centre
Splatts House
Heddington, Calne
Wiltshire SN11 0PE
Retreat House

Lanherne
Meaver Road
Mullion, Helston
Cornwall TR12 7DN
Bed & Breakfast

Lavender House
17 Bloomfield Park, Bath
Somerset BA2 2BY
Bed & Breakfast

Other Places and Organisations

School of the Living Light
Millslade Hall, Station Road
Ashcott, Bridgwater
Somerset TA7 9QP
Own Course Programme

Lower Norris House
North Huish, Totnes
Devon TQ10 9NJ
Bed & Breakfast

The Magdalen Project
Magdalen Farm
Winsham, Chard
Somerset TA20 4PA
Own Course Programme

Making Waves Organic Vegan Guesthouse
3 Richmond Place, St Ives
Cornwall TR26 1JN
© 01736 793895
Bed & Breakfast

Marlborough House
1 Marlborough Lane, Bath
Somerset BA1 2NQ
Bed & Breakfast

Marridge Hill Cottage
Marridge Hill
Ramsbury, Marlborough
Wiltshire SN8 2HG
Bed & Breakfast

Mill House Retreats
Rocknell Manor Farm
Westleigh
Tiverton
EX16 7ES
© 01884 829000
Retreat House

Mount Pleasant Farm
Gorran High Lanes, St Austell
Cornwall PL26 6LR
Bed & Breakfast

The Old Forge at Totnes
Seymour Place
Totnes
Devon TQ9 5AY
Bed & Breakfast

Pilgrims
12/13 Norbins Rd
Glastonbury
Somerset BA6 9JE
Bed & Breakfast

Pilsdon Community
Pilsdon Manor
Bridport
Dorset DT6 5NZ
Retreat House

Prebendal Farm
Bishopstone
Swindon
Wiltshire SN6 8PT
Bed & Breakfast

Really Useful Holidays
Causilgey Manor
Tregavethan, Truro
Cornwall TR4 9EP
Holiday Operator

Riverbank Hotel
45 Gold Street, Tiverton
Devon EX16 6QB
Health Spa

Running Waters
Porth Valley, Porth
Newquay
Cornwall TR8 4AW
Venue for hire

St Antoine Guest House
2 Guildhill Road
Southbourne
Bournemouth
Dorset BH6 3EY
Bed & Breakfast

Other Places and Organisations

Sancreed House
Sancreed
Penzance
Cornwall
TR20 8QS
Retreat House

**Sarpenela Natural
Therapy Centre**
Farnham Farm House
Farnham, Blandford
Dorset DT11 8DG
Health Spa

Schumacher College
The Old Postern
Dartington
Totnes
Devon TQ9 6EA
Own Course Programme

**Shambhala Health &
Healing Retreat**
Coursing Batch, Glastonbury
Somerset BA6 8BH
Retreat House

The Sheldon Centre
Dunsford
Exeter
Devon EX6 7LE
Venue for hire

Southcliffe
Lee Road, Lynton
Devon EX35 6BS
Bed & Breakfast

**Sparrowhawk Backpackers
Vegetarian Hostel**
45 Ford St, Moretonhampstead
Devon TQ13 8LN
✆ 01647 440318
Venue for Hire

Springhead Trust
Fontmell Magna
Shaftesbury
Dorset SP7 0NU
Venue for hire

Steps Farm
Wyke Champflower, Bruton
Somerset BA10 0PW
Own Course Programme

Tidicombe House
Arlington, Barnstaple
Devon
EX31 4SP
Venue for hire

**Tregoddick Farm
School of Yoga**
Tregoddick Farm,
Madron, Penzance
Cornwall TR20 8SS
Own Course Programme

Tribe of Doris
c/o 26 Albany Road
Montpelier
Bristol BS6 5LH
Camps

Whitesands Lodge
Sennen, Penzance
Cornwall TR19 7AR
Venue for hire

Woodlands Hotel
Pentire Crescent, Newquay
Cornwall TR17 1PU
Bed & Breakfast

The Yarner Trust
Welcombe Barton
Welcombe
Bideford
Devon
EX39 6HG
Venue for hire

South East England

Venues in
Berkshire
Buckinghamshire
East Sussex
Greater London
Hampshire
Isle of Wight
Kent
Oxfordshire
Surrey
West Sussex

◇ Redfield

OXFORD
Highfield West ◇
◇ Global Retreat
Charney Manor 94 ◆
St Ethelwold's ◆ **The Abbey 92** ◆
Woodrow 100
◆
St Peter's Bourne ◇
◇ 23 The Ridgeway
Braziers 93 ◆
Grail Centre ◇
44 Grove Road
LONDON
◇ 192 Regents Park Road
Temple Lodge ◇ ◆ Quaker International
Douai Abbey 97 ◆
◇ Emmaus
Eden Centre ◇ ◇ Barrow
Marie Reparatrice ◇
Tekels Park ◇ ◇ Ruth White
St Columba's
Four Winds ◇
◆ **Seekers 99**
◇ Centrespace
Stacklands ◇ ◇ The Friars
Commonwork 96 ◆ ◇ Oxon Hoath ◇ Tor Spa
SOUTHAMPTON
Claridge House 95 ◆ ◇ New Directions
Worth Abbey ◇ ◇ Burrswood
Park Place 98 ◆
St Cuthman's ◇ Emerson ◇ Hourne Farm
Hoffman Nash ◇ Priory of Our Lady
Marsh Farm ◇
14 Chatsworth Road
Granville Hotel
Haven ◇ ◇ Brambles Paskins ◇ Florence House

The Abbey

Sutton Courtenay
Abingdon
Oxfordshire
OX14 4AF
☎ 01235 847401
✆ 01235 847608
✍

admin@theabbeysc.demon.co.uk

✔ **Retreat House**
✔ **Bed & Breakfast**
✔ **Own Course Programme**
✔ **Venue for hire**
group full board (£35 to £50), group self catering, large indoor space, several small spaces
⌁ 18 bedspaces (6 singles.)
🍽 Exclusively vegetarian. Special diets catered for.
🚌 Didcot Station then bus 32 to The Triangle, Sutton Courtenay (or taxi – about £7)

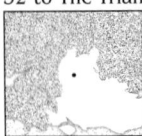

Focus
Inter-faith

The Abbey is a retreat and education centre housed in a 13th Century buildings and four acres of peaceful grounds. Rooted in the Christian tradition and open to the wisdom of other faiths, the Abbey provides a setting for the exploration of deep spiritual truths and values and the mystery of life. The community based at the Abbey, locally and further afield, holds a sacred space, open to this universal quest for truth.

The beauty and tranquillity of the house and grounds invite contemplation and a stilling of the inner. The challenges of living within an honest community of people whilst running a thriving education and retreat centre also encourage active engagement with the realities of modern life. We hold a welcome for all who are seeking to live life inspired by spirit.

Event Types
Guided group retreats, self directed retreats, business retreats, own course programme.

Subject Specialities
Group process, inner process, meditation, self expression, community living, emergent spirituality.

Eco-tourism features
The Abbey is just off the Sustrans cycle route No 5 between Oxford and Didcot.

Braziers Park was founded in 1950 as a practical centre to study humankind's place in the world. It is run by a resident group, and volunteers who donate their services. Braziers is set in 50 acres of graceful Chiltern countryside, with pasture and woodland, in an area of outstanding natural beauty. The main house itself is Grade 2* listed and is complemented by numerous outbuildings. Braziers estate is organic and the walled kitchen garden provides much of the produce for the house in season. Cooking is substantially, but not exclusively, vegetarian. The atmosphere is relaxed and informal.

Event Types

Guided group retreats, guided individual retreats, self directed retreats, business retreats, own course programme, working holidays.

Subject Specialities

Alternative lifestyles & technology, group process, inner process, food & gardening, arts & crafts, self expression, ritual & shamanic, meditation, body & breathwork, counselling, health and healing.

Suitability or Specialism

Adults, couples, women, men, older people.

Eco-tourism features

Permaculture.

Ipsden
Wallingford
Oxfordshire
OX10 6AN

☎ 01491 680221
📠 01491 680221
✉ admin@braziers.org.uk
✔ **Retreat House**
✔ **Bed & Breakfast**
✔ **Own Course Programme**
✔ **Venue for hire**
group full board (from £56), group self catering, large indoor space, several small spaces
🛏 31 bedspaces (3 singles, 4 twins, 3 doubles, 4 family rooms.)
🍽 Special diets.
♿ Ground floor only
🚖 Taxi from Goring & Streatley Railway Station.

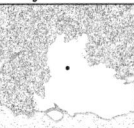

Charney Manor

The Manager, Charney Manor
Charney Bassett, Wantage
Oxfordshire OX12 0EJ
℡ 01235 868206
✆ 01235 868882
📠
charneymanor@quaker.org.uk
✔ **Retreat House**
✔ **Own Course Programme**
✔ **Venue for hire**
*group full board (£67.50),
group self catering, large and
small spaces*
🛏 42 bedspaces (12 twin,
10 single in the house and
annex; 8 in the Gilletts, self-
catering cottage) 14 of these
en-suite.
🍽 Special diets.
♿ Wheelchair access.
🚃 Train to Didcot Parkway
 then 20
minute taxi
journey.

Focus Quaker

Charney Manor, one of the
oldest inhabited houses in
Britain, is a place of tranquillity where people come for
reflection, renewal and retreat.
With its comfortable rooms
and delightful gardens, the
Manor, owned and managed
by Quakers (the Religious
Society of Friends), offers
a warm welcome to visitors
throughout the year. As well
as conferences and training
events for religious and other
groups, Charney hosts its own
programme of courses which
reflect current and emerging
concerns amongst Quakers.
These courses seek to nourish the spirit through silence,
listening deeply and exploring
with heart and mind (please
contact our office for our
current programme). Two of
our en-suite rooms have full
wheel-chair access and there

is a lift to our main meeting
room in the Barn. There is a
self-catering cottage in the
grounds (with 8 beds in 5 bedrooms) suitable for families
and small groups.

Event types
Guided group retreats, self-
directed retreats, residential

and day conference bookings.
Own course programme.
Subject specialities
Personal spiritual journeys,
seasonal retreats, creativity,
meditation and prayer, interfaith dialogue, justice and
peace witness.

Claridge House Healing Centre

Are you seeking a peaceful retreat from the bustle of the world?

Twice daily Quiet Time, two acres of gardens to roam in and a range of possible healing activities, is on offer at this haven for inner peace. Meditation, Massage, Voice work, Reiki, Circle Dancing, Creative writing, A Course in Miracles, T'ai Chi and Alexander Technique are just some of the wide range of subjects on offer.

Our programme of courses, to heal mind, body and spirit, can be sent to you on request. We are also being available to welcome those who prefer to arrange their own retreat.

Our Quiet Room houses the Friends Fellowship of Healing library, with a wide range of books on themes of Healing and Spirituality. Easily reached from London and the South East, this oasis for refreshment is also attractive to many people from much further afield.

Accommodation

20 beds (4 singles, 1 double and 7 twins) each with wash basin and drinks making facilities. Full board may be up to £50 per person per night, with reductions for certain Special Breaks, see our programme.

Event Types

Adult individual, couples or Group Retreats and a range of Courses

Subject Specialities

Healing in various forms, Rest and Renewal

Focus

Founded by Friends, but open to all faiths and none

Dormans Road, Dormansland Lingfield, Surrey RH7 6QH

℡ 01342 832150

📠 01342 836730

✉ welcome@ claridgehouse.quaker.eu.org

✔ **Retreat House**

✔ **Own Course Programme**

⌐ 20 bedspaces (4 singles, 7 twins, 1 double.)

🍽 Exclusively Vegetarian, with Vegan and other Special Diets catered for.

♿ Wheelchairs and suitable access is available to the four ground floor bedrooms, with a purpose built unit to suit those with disabilities.

🚆 Train from London Victoria to Lingfield, then walk or we meet you. Bus services nearby. Collection from Gatwick by arrangement.

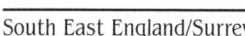

South East England/Surrey

The Commonwork Centre

Bore Place, Chiddingstone
Edenbridge, Kent TN8 7AR
✆ 01732 463255 x229
✆ 01732 740264
✉ info@commonwork.org
✔ **Retreat House**
✔ **Own Course Programme**
✔ **Venue for hire**
group full board (£76.38 to £144.53), group self catering (£44.65 to £50.53), large and small spaces
⌁ 45 bedspaces (7 singles, 15 twins, 3 family rooms.) Camping by arrangement.
🍽 Delicious meals, using local and organic ingredients where possible; self catering groups welcomed. Licensed, Fairtrade tea and coffee.
♿ Two meeting rooms and some residential accommodation are wheelchair accessible.
🚃 Train to Sevenoaks then taxi from station forecourt to Bore Place.

Commonwork, an educational trust, is a place for conferences, workshops and seminars on a 500-acre organic farm in the beautiful Kentish low Weald, near Sevenoaks. An old manor house (listed Grade II), with its ancient walled garden, and a group of historic barns within a courtyard, have been sensitively renovated to provide a restful but creative environment. Our variety of spaces means that we can accommodate small or large groups in comfort and with privacy, up to approx. 45 residents or 4 to 100 people for daytime visits. Each group has exclusive use of their space 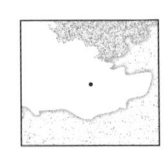 during their visit to undertake their own work or retreat. We

can also arrange Commonwork tutors for group activities such as claywork, guided walks, night walks, breadmaking and green woodwork. Our spaces are also suitable for dance, music and drama.
Our field trail through farmland and woodland – with 25 ponds – can be walked at any time and we also have a mini-field trail at the heart of the site which is wheelchair accessible.
Please do not hesitate to contact us about your specific requirements and budget. Prices are negotiable for not-for-profit groups.

Eco-tourism features
We run environmental education, garden and conservation programmes.

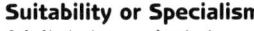

Douai Abbey

A Benedictine monastery offering hospitality and day conference facilities to individuals, small groups and workshops; also an organised retreat programme. Situated on the North Wessex Downs in an area of outstanding natural beauty. Good network of footpaths for walking. A variety of accommodation, some en suite. Meals are provided. Also available is hostel type self-catering accommodation. Further information about staying and about our retreat and workshop programme can be obtained from the Programme Director. Good rail and road connections: M4 exit 12 is 6 miles: railway station Midgham on Paddington to Newbury line is 1 mile. Oxford, Stonehenge and Winchester all within an hour's drive.

Event Types
Guided group retreats, self directed retreats, business retreats, own course programme.

Subject Specialities
Meditation, prayer.

Suitability or Specialism
Adults(+), couples(+), families with children, women, men, young people 12 to 17, children under 12, older people.

Focus Christian/Catholic

Fr Oliver Holt, Douai Abbey
Upper Woolhampton, Reading
Berkshire RG7 5TQ
℅ 0118 971 5399
℅ 0118 971 5303
✆ info@douaiabbey.org.uk
✔ **Retreat House**
✔ **Holiday Operator**
✔ **Own Course Programme**
✔ **Venue for hire**
group full board (£35 to £43), group self catering, large and small spaces
↝ 46 bedspaces (18 singles, 2 twins, 1 double, 1 family room, 5 dormitories.)
🍽 Special diets.
♿ All public areas: churches, refectories, conference rooms, but not residential rooms (full access building programme about to start).
🚆 Midgham Station 1 mile away – walk or take taxi.

Park Place Pastoral Centre

http://www.parkplacepastoralcentre.co.uk

Wickham, Fareham
Hampshire PO17 5HA
℡ 01329 833043
✆ 01329 832226
✆ parkplacecentre@aol.com
✔ **Retreat House**
✔ **Own Course Programme**
✔ **Venue for hire**
*group full board, group self
catering, large & small spaces*
↝ 60 beds, in 47 rooms,
(28 rooms en-suite). Separate,
self contained Youth Wing,
catering for 25 young people
plus 5 leaders also available.
♿ Wheelchair access to the
dining room, meeting rooms,
chapel and a limited number
of ground floor bedrooms.
🚌 Train and National Express
services to
Portsmouth,
Winchester
and Fareham.
Then bus to
Wickham.

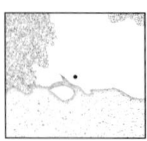

The Pastoral Centre is
a unique and attrac-
tive location run by the
Franciscan Sisters of St
Mary of the Angels, situated
near Wickham, a charming
Hampshire village midway
between Southampton,
Portsmouth & Winchester. It
offers a location where people
of all Faiths, or none, can
come together to develop their
values helped by a temporary
withdrawal from the purely
material demands of every day
life and relax in a peaceful and
calm environment.
150 seater conference room,
(with PA.) 3 smaller meeting
rooms, a large dining room
and a modern, simple chapel.
All levels of catering from B&B
to full board, for single days to
full weeks. Simple vegetarian
meals can be provided.
2 rooms on ground floor for
disabled guests and carers.
ASSISI HOUSE, which can
accommodate ten people in
2 twin bedded and 6 single
bedded en-suite rooms, is a
modern annexe to the Pastoral
Centre. Assisi House offers an
ideal facility for family, group
or individual holidays, with
many cultural, historic and
religious attractions within a
short bus or car drive. Groups
and individuals are welcome
to take meals in the Centre's
dining room or prepare their
own meals in the modern well-
equipped kitchen in Assisi
House. A separate, self catering, Youth Wing can accommodate 30 people.

Event Types
Organised retreats and days
of recollection; Guests own
retreats, meetings & courses;
Holidays.

Subject Specialities
Sadhana Meditation & Yoga,
painting and calligraphy,
Indian cooking.

Focus All faith communities
and lay groups

The Seekers Trust

For over 75 years The Seekers Trust has been a centre for prayer and spiritual healing. A warm welcome awaits those who seek an informal retreat and/or spiritual healing. Through the harmony prayer circles thousands experiencing health, emotional and material problems have found help and gained new hope, thanks to our unique system of Christian prayer.

Accommodation
We have 5 single and 3 double (twin-bedded) self-catering flats. All with double glazing, central heating. Bed linen and towels are provided. We are open all year round.

Other facilities
Conference, workshop and seminar facilities also available with ample car parking nearby.

Event Programme
Events are organised by outside bodies. Diary available upon request.

Subject Specialities
Annual healing course run by Resident Trainer.

Suitability
Adults

Eco-tourism features
Set in 39 acres of parkland amid the beautiful Kent countryside, with our own woodland walks.

The Close
Addington Park
West Malling
Kent
ME19 5BL

℃ 01732 843589
℡ 01732 842867

theseekerstrust@supanet.com

✔ **Retreat House**
✔ **Venue for hire**
⤷ 5 single flats and 3 twin-bedded flats.
♿ Limited wheelchair access at present but improvements planned.
🚃 West Malling railway station, then 10 minute taxi ride.

Focus
Non-denominational centre for absent and contact healing through the power of prayer.

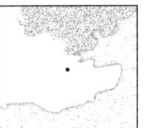

Woodrow High House

http://www.woodrow-high.co.uk

Roy Hickman
Woodrow High House
Cherry Lane
Woodrow
Amersham
Buckinghamshire
HP7 0QG
✆ 01494 433531
📠 01494 431391

linda.collins@woodrow-high.co.uk

✔ **Retreat House**
✔ **Venue for hire**
group full board, large indoor space, several small spaces
⤴ 53 bedspaces (1 single, 13 twins, 7 family rooms.)
🍽 Special diets.
♿ Wheelchair access.
🚃 Train to Amersham then taxi to Woodrow High House.

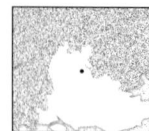

Woodrow High House is a historic listed building set in beautiful landscaped grounds and has a unique atmosphere. Woodrow's extensive facilities offer almost unlimited possibilities to visiting groups for their programme requirements. Residential bookings always represent good value providing shared accommodation for up to 53 visitors. There are large meeting rooms and lounge areas all furnished in a traditional style. The games room and arts and crafts rooms are popular venues for relaxation and learning.

Recreation, leisure and creative activities including the performing arts are well catered for in Woodrow's splendid new sports complex. There is a heated indoor swimming pool, showers, and changing rooms, a fully adaptable sports hall/auditorium with theatre stage plus recording and rehearsal rooms. Woodrow High House is owned and managed by The Federation of London Youth Clubs.

Event Types
Self directed retreats.

Subject Specialities
Outdoor activities & sport, arts & crafts.
Suitability or Specialism
Adults, families with children, women, men, young people 12 to 17, children under 12, older people.

Other Places and Organisations

14 Chatsworth Road B&B
Brighton
East Sussex
BN1 5DB
℗ 01273 556584
Bed & Breakfast

23 The Ridgeway B&B
Finchley
London
N3 2PG
Bed & Breakfast

44 Grove Road B&B
Finchley
London
N12 9DX
Bed & Breakfast

192 Regents Park Rd B&B
Primrose Hill, London
NW1 8XP
Bed & Breakfast

Barrow House
45 Barrow Road
Streatham Common
London
SW16 5PE
Bed & Breakfast

Brambles
10 Clarence Road
Shanklin
Isle of Wight
PO37 7BH
Bed & Breakfast

Burrswood
Groombridge
Tunbridge Wells
Kent
TN3 9PY
Retreat House

Centrespace
3 Alcroft Grange, Tyler Hill
Canterbury, Kent CT2 9NN
Retreat House

Eden Centre
252 Kingston Road
Teddington
Middlesex
TW11 9JQ
Retreat House

Emerson College
Forest Row, East Sussex
RH18 5JX
℗ 01342 822238
Own Course Programme

Other Places and Organisations

The Emmaus Centre
Layhams Road
West Wickham, Kent
BR4 9HH
✆ 020 8777 2000
Retreat House

Florence House
Southdown Road
Seaford
East Sussex
BN25 4JS
Venue for hire

Four Winds Centre
High Thicket Road
Dockenfield, Farnham
Surrey GU10 4HE
Venue for hire

The Friars
Aylesford Priory
Aylesford
Kent
ME20 7BX
Venue for hire

Global Retreat Centre
Nuneham Park
Nuneham Courtney
Oxford OX44 9PG
Own Course Programme

The Grail Centre
125 Waxwell Lane, Pinner
Middlesex HA5 3ER
✆ 020 8866 0505
Retreat House

Granville Hotel
124 Kings Road, Brighton
East Sussex BN1 2FA
Bed & Breakfast

The Haven
St Boniface Road
Ventnor
Isle of Wight
PO38 1PL
Retreat House

Highfield West B&B
188 Cumnor Hill
Oxford
OX2 9PJ
Bed & Breakfast

Hoffman Institute
The Old Post House
Burpham
Arundel
West Sussex
BN18 9RH
✆ 01903 889990
Own Course Programme

Other Places and Organisations

Hourne Farm
Steel Cross, Crowborough
East Sussex TN6 2SQ
Venue for hire

Marie Reparatrice
115 Ridgway, Wimbledon
London SW19 4RB
Retreat House

Marsh Farm Centre and Retreat
Binsted
Arundel
West Sussex
BN18 0LH
Own Course Programme

Nash Manor
Horsham Road
Steyning
West Sussex
BN44 3AA
Bed & Breakfast

Centre of New Directions
White Lodge
Stockland Green Road
Speldhurst
Tunbridge Wells
Kent
TN3 0TT
Retreat House

Priory of Our Lady of Good Counsel
Sayers Common
Hassocks
West Sussex
BN6 9HT
Retreat House

Oxon Hoath
Hadlow
Tonbridge
Kent
TN11 9SS
Venue for hire

Paskins Town House
18/19 Charlotte Street
Brighton, East Sussex
BN2 1AG
Bed & Breakfast

Quaker International Centre
1-3 Byng Place, Bloomsbury
London WC1E 7JH
Bed & Breakfast

Redfield Centre
Buckingham Road
Winslow
Buckingham
MK18 3LZ
Own Course Programme

Other Places and Organisations

Ruth White Yoga Centre
Church Farm House
Springclose Lane
Cheam
Surrey
SM3 8PU
Own Course Programme

St Columba's House
Maybury Hill
Woking
Surrey
GU22 8AB
© 01483 766498
Retreat House

St Cuthmans
Coolham
Horsham
West Sussex
RH13 8QL
Retreat House

St Ethelwold's
30 East St Helen's Street
Abingdon
Oxfordshire
OX14 5EB
Retreat House

**St Peter's Bourne
Christian Education and
Spirituality Centre**
40 Oakleigh Park South
Whetsone
London
N20 9JN
© 020 8445 5535
Retreat House

Stacklands Retreat House
School Lane
West Kingsdown
Sevenoaks
Kent
TN15 6AN
Retreat House

Tekels Park Guest House
Tekels Park Estate
Camberley, Surrey
GU15 2LF
© 01276 23159
Bed & Breakfast

Temple Lodge
The Gate
51 Queen Caroline Street
Hammersmith
London
W6 9QL
Bed & Breakfast

Tor Spa Retreat
Ickham
Canterbury
Kent
CT3 1QN

**Worth Abbey Centre
for Spirituality**
Turners Hill
Crawley
West Sussex
RH10 4SB
Retreat House

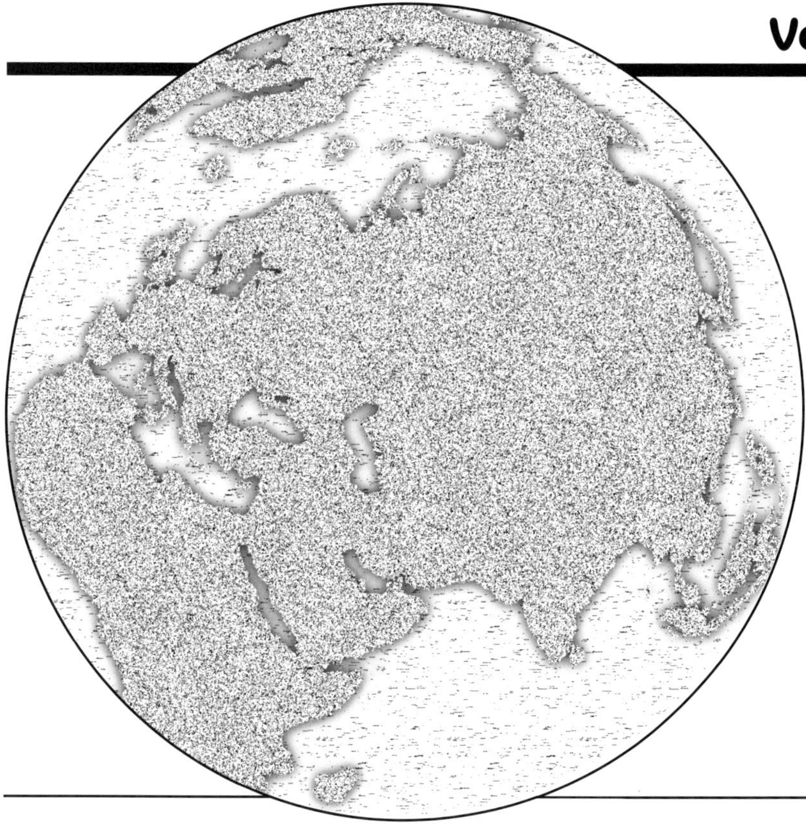

Venues outside the UK

Venues in
Barbados
France
Germany
Greece
India
Ireland
Italy
Portugal
Spain
Sri Lanka
Turkey

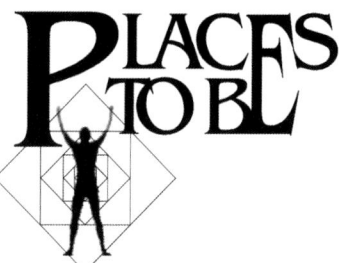

The Sanctuary Barbados

http://thesanctuarybarbados.com

Gay Taaffe and Jaclyn Bailey
The Sanctuary
Chimborazo House
St Joseph
Barbados

© 00 1 246 433 1787
✆ 00 1 246 433 1787

info@thesanctuarybarbados.com

✔ **Retreat House**
✔ **Holiday Operator**
✔ **Own Course Programme**
✔ **Venue for hire**
group full board, group self catering, large indoor space

Begin your search for inner peace surrounded by positive energies.
Located in Chimborazo, the first part of the island to emerge from the ocean two million years ago, The Sanctuary is built over ancient crystal laced coral rocks. Through these amazing rocks you can tap into your powerful divine source. Stress and worries will simply slip away when you are empowered by your own soul purpose.
Our Program Includes
- Weekly itinerary inclusive of workshops, yoga and therapies.
- Full board accommodation in our elegant 18th century residence.

- International guest tutors.
- Two centre options.
For more information visit our web site.

Le Blé en Herbe

Le Blé en Herbe is a small, international holistic retreat with 7.5 acres of beautiful organic gardens, fields, woods, a large converted barn and farm guesthouse. Le Blé is located in central France in the gently rolling foothills of the Massif Central, a haven for wild flowers, butterflies and birds of prey. Visitors are offered a variety of refreshing holiday options in a nurturing, nourishing atmosphere. Delicious vegetarian/vegan meals are prepared with organic produce fresh daily from the "Sun" Garden. Produce for sale to self-catering guests. We offer B&B, full board, self-catering "Rose Cottage" (sleeps 2-4 people), camping and courses (herbalism, massage, dance, pottery). Nearest station is Guéret. Caen, Dieppe and Le Havre are 300 miles. Bookings only, maximum number of guests is 20.

Event Types
Guided group retreats, own course programme, working holidays.

Subject Specialities
Food & gardening, alternative lifestyles & technology, health & healing, arts & crafts, inner process, group process, earth mysteries.

Suitability or Specialism
Adults.

Eco-tourism features
Permaculture, solar and wind power (small scale), living willow structures.

Maria Sperring
Le Blé en Herbe
Puissetier
La Cellette
FR-23350
France

✆ 00 33 5 55806283
✆ 00 33 5 55806283
☞

maria.sperring@gofornet.com
✔ **Bed & Breakfast**
✔ **Own Course Programme**
✔ **Venue for hire**
group full board, large indoor space, several small spaces
⌁ 17 bedspaces (3 singles, 4 twins, 6 doubles.)
🍽 Exclusively vegetarian, special diets.
🚃 Train from Paris to Châteauroux or bus from London to Limoges then train to Guéret. Collection by arrangement.
Focus Eco-spirituality

La Buissière

Duravel
FR-46700
France

© 00 33 565 36 43 51
℡ 00 33 565 36 43 47
✉ labuissiere@wanadoo.fr

✔ **Retreat House**
✔ **Holiday Operator**
✔ **Venue for hire**
group self catering
↰ 10 bedspaces (4 twins,
1 double)
♿ All facilities on one level
– except some studios
🚃 Cahors Railway Station
then regular bus service to
stop outside

Step out of your daily routine and into the rural tranquillity of the beautiful Lot valley in SW France. Nourish body and mind with a week of well-being and relaxation, with gentle hatha yoga, guided walks, massage, sightseeing and great gastronomy.

Yoga and Walking

Anybody and everybody, young and old, can benefit from yoga at La Buissière, which is suitable for both beginners and as 'holiday maintenance' for regular practitioners. It is an excellent area for rambling and exploring, largely unspoilt and steeped in history. Ancient footpaths and bridleways criss-cross wooded hillsides and vineyards with magnificent views and riverside walks.

Accommodation

Set in 2 acres of private parkland with large pool, the centre has been carefully restored and specially customised to a very high standard. Group sizes are limited to a maximum of 10 guests staying in mainly twin bedded studios, each with its own fully equipped kitchenette, private en-suite facilities and separate WC. Treat yourself to a massage, chill out in a hammock or get out and about and discover the colour and gastronomy of this unique and fascinating part of France. Particularly suitable for Adults aged 18 and above.

Eco-tourism features

We encourage water conservation, waste recycling and low energy consumption. Chemical-free pool. All support services are sourced locally and local businesses all benefit from our patronage.

Spacebetween

If you're looking for that elusive balance between tranquillity, accessibility and choice of amenities, then the Vésubie valley in the Mercantour National Park is that "Holy Grail" – an undiscovered "spacebetween" the hustle and bustle of the Côte d'Azur and the well trodden areas in the Alps to the North, and all just one hour away from Nice.

We are British outdoor enthusiasts with many years experience of walking, climbing and global travel. We organise walking holidays, with hotel accommodation in St Martin Vésubie and our own gîte accommodation. You can of course join us with accommodation only at La Zourcière, recently awarded "2 wheatsheaf" Gîtes de France status. We are also able to "tailor make" breaks - perhaps including some time on the Côte d'Azur.

La Zourcière at Berthemont-les-Bains is situated at 860m with enviable 360 degree views. Its six acres of land enjoy an abundance of bird and animal life, enabling guests to "observe" from the comfort of a sunny terrace or to strike out on foot on the many paths around the house.

Within the house there is a self-contained gîte with bedroom/living room – kitchen - bathroom and separate bedroom – private terrace - for 4/5 people plus 1 double ensuite B&B room. The local town of Roquebillière offers a selection of friendly bars and restaurants.

Access

SpaceBetween will actively be seeking to promote holidays for wheelchair users in the Mercantour.

Eco-tourism

We use the wealth of organic product available in the hamlet of Berthemont-les-Bains, and encourage guests to offer nothing but respect to the Park, through pre visit information. We support a local sanctuary aiming to re-introduce the wolf to the Mercantour.

Liz Lord
Spacebetween
PO Box 893
Hazlemere
High Wycombe
Buckinghamshire
HP15 7XZ

© 0870 243 0667
℡ 0870 243 0667
✉ liz@space-between.co.uk

✔ **Bed & Breakfast**
✔ **Holiday Operator**
✔ **Retreat House**

⤴ Our own accommodation plus that of our hotel partners.

✈ Nice Airport then our own transport.

The Sun Centre

Sharon Black
The Sun Centre
La Source
Prades
St Martin de Boubaux
FR-48160
France
ⓒ 00 33 4 66 45 59 63
✆ retreat@thesuncentre.com

✔ **Retreat House**
✔ **Bed & Breakfast**
✔ **Own Course Programme**
✔ **Venue for hire**
group full board (£35 to £38), group self catering, large indoor space, several small spaces
🍽 Exclusively vegetarian.
♿ Not suitable for people with walking difficulties (no wheelchair access, some steps and uneven ground).
🚆 Train (TGV) or aeroplane to Montpellier or Nîmes. Then train, bus or shared taxi to Alès.

The Sun Centre is a holistic retreat offering themed holidays, rest and recuperation in the beautiful Cévennes mountains of the Languedoc region of France. Specialities: yoga, Ayurveda and Louise Hay personal development. Open Retreats for guests wishing to set their own agenda are also possible.

Surrounded by pine and chestnut forests, the centre is located in a tiny hamlet (accessible by footpath only) 2 hours from Nîmes / Montpellier. Close by, the river Galeizon meanders across the valley floor, providing a multitude of shimmering bathing spots in summer. There is excellent walking, hiking and wild-camping just minutes up the hillside. Horses can be hired from an equestrian centre 15 mins away.

The area is abundant in wildlife. Buzzards, falcons, pheasants, woodpeckers and even eagles can be glimpsed or heard among the trees. The valley is also a favourite haunt of wild boar, badgers, deer and other woodland animals.

Workshop spaces include an outdoor yoga deck, a glass-fronted cabin, a spacious converted loft and our lovely Mongolian yurt. Accommodation is provided in simple but comfortable twin rooms. Single rooms, dorms and camping discounts are available.

Meals are delicious, homemade, vegetarian and inspired by the ancient life-wisdom of Ayurveda. Most of our ingredients are organic and many of the vegetables are grown in the hamlet.

Optional extras include massage, reflexology, Ayurvedic consultations, craniosacral therapy, life counselling and private yoga tuition.

Eco-tourism features
Mongolian yurt, local organic produce, compost toilets.

Gaia Visions Retreat Zakynthos

Located in the beautiful pristine peninsula of Vassilicos, Gaia Visions Retreat is a cultural and self-development centre. It is a place where you can learn and experience the real Greece, as well as have fun, take time for yourself and reconnect with nature and your own inner beauty.
We offer morning yoga and meditation, massage, nature walks and excursions plus the opportunity to take Greek dancing and/or self development courses. We can also organise horse-riding, ceramic-making, para-gliding, water-sports and mosaics. Accommodation is situated near to the beautiful beach of Gerakas – where the rare spe-

cies of Loggerhead Turtle, the Caretta-Caretta, comes to rest. Participants are welcome to share and contribute in the running of this small, friendly community retreat. Accommodation is on a shared room basis unless otherwise requested. We specialise in offering all-inclusive programmes starting from £375 per person per week.

Event Types
Guided group retreats, guided individual retreats, business retreats.

Subject Specialities
Yoga, meditation, self development, health & healing, body & breathwork, self expression, outdoor activities & sport, counselling.

Suitability or Specialism
Adults, couples, lesbian women, gay men, women, men, older people.

Frances Engelhardt
36 Woodstock Avenue
Sutton
Surrey
SM3 9EF

✆ 020 8401 8319
✉ gaiavisions@yahoo.com

✔ **Retreat House**
✔ **Holiday Operator**
⌁ 12 bedspaces (4 twins, 2 doubles.)
🍴 Exclusively vegetarian.
✈ Flight direct to Zakynthos, pick-up included in price. Alternatively bus and local flight connections from Athens – travel assistance given.

Focus Eco-spirituality

White Mountain Retreat

Julie Murray Franks
25 Roman Road
Hove
East Sussex
BN3 4LB

© 01273 416050

info@whitemountainretreat.com

✔ **Retreat House**
✔ **Holiday Operator**
✔ **Own Course Programme**
✔ **Venue for hire**
group full board (£35 to £60), group self catering, large indoor space, several small spaces
⤴ 20 bedspaces (2 singles, 5 twins, 2 doubles, 1 family room.)
🍽 Special diets.
✈ Flights to Chania airport then 45 min by WMR car. Flights to Heraklion then taxi 2 hours or Bus by day 3 hours.

Much of what is available here in Crete at White Mountain Retreat is simple and God-given. Yet in this world where spin, speed and stress can make even the hardiest soul dizzy, maybe we can grasp this opportunity of quiet and space to breathe, enjoy and just Be. In offering simple retreat holidays and a selection of inspiring courses we consider your time with us to be precious. Our aim is to nourish and support your enjoyment in mind body and spirit.

We have a superb coastal situation surrounded by olive groves enjoying breathtaking views of sea, sky and mountains with a wonderful presence of healing energy.

A Time to Learn, A Time to Experience. A Time to Be Who You Really Are. Send for our Brochure for more details. Our phone number in Greece is 0030 28250 32028.

Focus Eco-spirituality

Eco-tourism features
Organic farming and gardening; working to permaculture; solar panels.

Beach and Lake Ayurvedic Resort

The Beach & Lake is a small (eight-roomed) privately owned Ayurvedic Resort, 8 km south of Trivandrum International Airport. It's nestled between the Arabian Sea and a river, situated on an island and blessed by nature. Access to the resort is only by private boat. Relax and receive the full benefit that such proximity to nature provides. All the bedrooms have verandas with a beach and lake view.

Ayurveda

Ayurveda is a health science, one of the oldest and most complete healing systems known. The word Ayurveda, derived from 2 Sanskrit terms, literally means the knowledge of life.

At the heart of Ayurveda lies the concept of three 'doshas': Kapha, Pitha and Vatha. Balancing the three harmoniously will promote a healthy body and mind. This holistic treatment system involves various types of massage and oil applications, inhalations, diet, and natural medicines as required.

Ayurveda Package

Chose from a number of treatment programmes, including slimming, purification (detox), rejuvenation, and stress management with yoga. The inclusive package is for consultation and a daily treatment, plus full board and accommodation in twin rooms.

Private Hire

The resort is also available for private hire and would suit groups of 14 or less. There are various outdoor spaces suitable for yoga, t'ai chi, and art or dance type work shops.
Per day: £200 (min 1 week)
Full Board @ £5.00 per person
Tours, cultural entertainment evenings and Ayurvedic massage can be arranged as required.

Eco-tourism features

Resort blends with local nature. All staff are local.

Pozhikkara Beach
Pachalloor PO
Trivandrum
Kerala
27
India

© 00 91 471 2382086
℡ 00 91 471 2382066
✍
beachandlake@hotmail.com

✔ **Retreat House**
✔ **Holiday Operator**
✔ **Own Course Programme**
✔ **Venue for hire**
group full board
↳ 16 bedspaces (8 twin rooms).
⦿ Special diets catered for.
✈ Trivandrum Airport then 20 minute taxi transfer provided

Focus Ayurveda

Fridays Place

http://www.fridaysplace.biz

Mark Reynolds
Fridays Place
Poovar Island
Poovar
Kerala
India

© 01428 741510
✆ 01428 741510
✆ letschill@fridaysplace.biz

✔ **Retreat House**
✔ **Holiday Operator**
✔ **Own Course Programme**
✔ **Venue for hire**
group full board, group self catering
⌒ 3 doubles.
🍽 Special diets.
♿ Wheelchair access under construction.
🚍 Trivandrum Airport then complimentary pickup
Focus Eclectic mix of Gautama, Gibran, Osho and Richard Bach

Fridays Place is an exclusive and private hideaway for the alternative in you. Just three beautifully crafted teak and mahogany cottages set in fifty acres of unspoilt palm garden, and on the banks of the quiet Neyyar Backwater, ensures a serene getaway far from the madding crowd. Alternative? Yes! We are only practically accessed by boat and have no neighbours for a half kilometre. We are the coolest on the Kerala coast. Surrounded by water, shady palms and acacia, temperatures are near perfect and as a real boon, there are no mosquitoes. Fridays Place is here for you to wonder, to chill, or just be! The food is organic and as you like ... South Indian at its best! If you can break away from your verandah or sunbathing under the palms in your hammock, then trips out to Kovalam beach are easily sorted; or for the more adventurous, jaunts out to the hills, rubber plantations, cashew nut factories and temples can be arranged. We heartily recommend a bit of a tour, and if you have time, we

can take in over a five day trip the amazing Meenakshi temple at Madurai, the Hill Station of Kodaikanal and the lush Tea Gardens of Munnar.
For the holistically minded, we are situated in the heart of Ayurveda country. Poovar Island Resort and Isola Di Cocco are neighbours a slow boat ride down river and we are able to arrange a competitive treatment regime with them during your stay.
Our small complex is available for sole booking and is ideal for like-minded friends to enjoy or a family reunion. The contemporary jungle aesthetic of our buildings with palm garden and river back drop make it the perfect location for media shoots.
UK Address: c/o Wispers, Titty Hill, Midhurst GU29 0PN
Do check out our website. You're nearly there!
Eco-tourism features
In constructing Fridays Place we have made minimal intrusion on our habitat. Completely solar powered and thoughtfully laid out, it is a haven for bird life and those who would wish to 'escape'.

Chrysalis Holistic Centre

Restful rural setting in Ireland (one hour south of Dublin) for homely holistic centre, specialising in residential workshops in many aspects of personal growth and spirituality, with facilities for private group bookings. Converted 18th century rectory and wooden chalet plus two delightful, comfortable octagonal hermitages situated in silent Zen meditation garden, both available for private retreats. Sauna, craft shop, organic garden, delicious meals, firm mattresses and a friendly red setter dog! We produce a biannual varied programme of events, available on request and we look forward to welcoming you to Ireland.

Event Types
Self directed retreats, own course programme, regeneration programmes.

Subject Specialities
Body & breathwork, counselling, group proc-ess, inner process, meditation.

Suitability or Specialism
Adults.

Claire Harrison
Chrysalis Holistic Centre
Donard
County Wicklow
Ireland

© 00 353 45 404713
℡ 00 353 45 404713
✆ peace@chrysalis.ie

✔ **Retreat House**
✔ **Own Course Programme**
✔ **Venue for hire**
group full board, group self catering, several small spaces
➴ 20 bedspaces (3 singles.)
⦿ Exclusively vegetarian, special diets.

Focus Ecumenical

Cloona Health Centre

Dhara Kelly
Cloona Health Centre
Westport
County Mayo
Ireland

✆ 00 353 98 25251
✉ info@cloona.ie

✔ **Retreat House**
✔ **Own Course Programme**
↪ 10 bedspaces (10 singles.)
🍽 Exclusively vegetarian.
♿ No wheelchair access.
🚗 Knock Airport or train to Westport then taxi.

Focus Celtic

When Cloona first opened its doors in 1973 we launched the concept of Health Tourism in Ireland. Our courses, both five-day (Sunday to Friday) and three-day (Thursday to Sunday) are exclusively residential. This, together with a quiet, rural location, ensures full privacy for our guests to enjoy what is intrinsically an experience in relaxation, self-care and de-toxifying. An energising, holistic programme, it consists of daily yoga, walks, sauna and massage and is based on a light, cleansing diet of fruit and vegetables that accords with the principles of proper food-combining. We have our own natural spring water on tap and are committed to the use of organic and GM-free produce.
Cloona is situated three miles from Westport, beside Croagh Patrick and Clew Bay.
Detox courses: 5-day (Sunday to Friday) €495; 3-day (Thursday to Sunday) €315

Event Types
Guided individual retreats, own course programme, programmes for healing and recovery.
Subject Specialities
Health & healing.
Suitability or Specialism
Adults.

Dunderry Park Transpersonal Centre

The Centre is situated in the heart of historic County Meath, close to the ancient sacred sites of Tara, Newgrange and Loughcrew, 45 minutes from Dublin airport. It is surrounded by 25 acres of wooded parkland. The house is a 250 year old Georgian residence which has been completely restored. There is, at present, shared accommodation for 32. The workroom is 41x19ft. Food is quality vegetarian. The Centre is available for hire to groups (minimum 18) for days, weekends or longer, at a cost of €65 per person per day, food and accommodation included. For further information on hiring the Centre or for a brochure on courses, please write or phone.

Event Types
Own course programme.

Subject Specialities
Body & breathwork, ritual & shamanic, holotropic breathwork, dance, yoga.

Annette Peard
Dunderry Park
Navan
County Meath
Ireland
℗ 00 353 46 9074455
℘ 00 353 46 9074455
dunderry@online.ie

✔ **Retreat House**
✔ **Holiday Operator**
✔ **Own Course Programme**
✔ **Venue for hire**
group full board (€65), large indoor space, several small spaces

↗ 32 bedspaces (1 single, 3 twins, 1 double, 4 family rooms, 1 dormitory.) Camping for 8-12.

🍴 Exclusively vegetarian. Special diets.

♿ Slide chair for stairs.

🚌 Bus to Navan, then taxi to Dunderry Park, or taxi direct from Dublin or the airport.

Focus Multi-denominational

Ealaín Uisce Healing Centre

✦ http://www.ealainuisce.net

Felicity Egan
Ealaín Uisce
Cushleaca
Mulranny
County Mayo
Ireland

✆ 00 353 98 36946
✝ ealainuisce@eircom.net

✔ Own Course Programme
✔ Venue for hire
group full board (up to £44)
⤳ 8 bedspaces (2 twins,
1 double.)
🍽 Exclusively vegetarian.
♿ Wheelchair access at front
door and 1 bedroom.
🚆 Knock Airport or train to
Westport then 18 miles by taxi
or collection by appointment

Ealaín Uisce was created as a place of retreat in which to develop mind, body and spirit in a tranquil and peaceful environment where healing can begin.

The centre nestles on the wild shores of Clew Bay in Co. Mayo. The rise and fall of the tides is a stone's throw away, with Croagh Patrick towering in the distance. Designed to harmonise with the breath-taking landscape.

The Venue
Four beautifully appointed en suite bedrooms can accommodate up to eight people comfortably for residential courses. All cooking will be vegetarian.
1000 sq ft studio with an attractive conservatory area. Two acres of secluded grounds. Spacious living / dining room area, flooded with natural light and warmed by an open fire. Massage room, meditation room.

Run Your Own Workshop
The centre can be hired by anyone wishing to run their own workshop or residential programme. The massage room can be rented out by practitioners on a daily or weekly basis: contact the centre for further information and rates.

Surroundings
Mulranny is a peaceful seaside village. With its rambling hills and trails, the area is ideal for hill walking. It has wonderful sandy beaches, one of which is suitable for swimming, and is a blue flag beach.

Situated on the south side of the Dingle Peninsula (R561), the Phoenix is a restored farmhouse with two acres of organic garden. Backed by the beautiful Slieve Mish Mountains and facing Castlemaine Harbour, there is plenty of scope for hill-walk-

ing. We have en-suite family rooms, hostel camping and a beautiful chalet to offer. There is an on site restaurant, serving organic vegetarian meals from breakfast to dinner time. We use our own home grown salads and herbs, plus a rich selection of locally produced foods, such as organic goats' feta and yoghurts. We cater for special diets. The emphasis is on a relaxed family run atmosphere. We are child friendly and pet friendly. See our website. B&B price €35/person shared, 50% single supplement.

We also have a traditional barrelcot gypsy caravan to let – sleeps four.

Event Types
Own course programme.

Subject Specialities
Meditation, inner process, alternative lifestyles & technology, food & gardening, outdoor activities & sport, conservation work, health & healing, body & breathwork, self expression.

Eco-tourism features
We work 2 acres of organic garden and use reedbed sewage.

Lorna or William
The Phoenix
Shanahill East
Castlemaine
County Kerry
Ireland

© 00 353 669 766284
✆ 00 353 669 766284
✉ phoenixtyther@hotmail.com

✔ **Bed & Breakfast**
✔ **Own Course Programme**
⌁ 15-20 bedspaces including chalet which sleeps family of 2-4 and costs from €450/week.
🍽 Exclusively vegetarian, special diets.
♿ Wheelchair access.
🚌 Buses run past house in summer months.

Moinhos Velhos

Frank Jensen
Moinhos Velhos
Cotifo
Lagos
PT-8600
Portugal

℃ 00 351 282 687 147
(00 351 282 687 697
✆ fasting@ip.pt

✔ **Holiday Operator**
✔ **Own Course Programme**
⌐ 12 bedspaces (4 singles, 4 twins.)
🍽 Exclusively vegetarian.

Focus New Age

Moinhos Velhos is a beautiful valley on the Algarve coast in Portugal. Inspired by the work of Drs Gerson and Bernard Jensen we offer the ultimate detoxification, purification and intestinal cleansing fasting program with juices and herbs. Transformation on the physical level is not our sole aim, but also on the emotional, mental and spiritual level. Thus we include yoga, meditation, therapeutic massage, Kinesiology and Bioresonance therapy as well as elimination of heavy metals and ACTS (the Automatic Computerised Treatments System). When we are not conducting a fasting program the facilities and services at Moinhos Velhos are available for other groups.

Event Types
Own course programme.

Subject Specialities
Health & healing.

Cortijo Arunachala

Located at 6,000 feet altitude in the spectacular Sierra Nevada Natural Park with views of snow-capped peaks to the north and of the Mediterranean to the south, Cortijo Arunachala is truly isolated from the business of every day life. We offer silent retreats between May and September to sincere spiritual practitioners who are 'open' to Self-enquiry. Group Silent Retreats are held once a month between May and August. Each retreat comprises 2 days' preparation, 7 days of silence (aside from satsang and guided meditations in the Tradition of the Himalayan Masters of which Nandini is an initiate) and ending with a final review day.

Cortijo Arunachala seeks to operate as a community based on the example of Bhagavan Sri Ramana Maharshi (1879-1950), known in India as 'the sage of Arunachala'. Ramana taught in silence, sought no disciples and respected all living creatures equally. Godfrey and Nandini welcome individuals who seek knowledge through silence and who enjoy sharing and working in an eco-spiritual environment. The low daily charge for full-board (vegetarian) is based upon all residents contributing to the preparation of food, cleaning and other community tasks. It is possible for participants to stay for a longer or shorter period if they wish. Participants must be able to live at altitude (1850m). With the arrival of Easy Jet in Granada it is now even easier to reach Granada than before.
UK Address (Sep to Mar):
36 Windmill Hill Road,
Glastonbury BA6 8EQ.
01458 835634

Eco-tourism features
Own mountain water supply, own solar powered electricity, own organic vegetable garden.

Nandini & Godfrey
Cortijo Arunachala
16 Calle Moraleda
Mondujar
Granada
ES-18656
Spain

℡ 00 34 677 958 788341
✉ bishop@
arunachala.fsworld.co.uk

✔ **Retreat House**
✔ **Own Course Programme**
🍽 Exclusively vegetarian
♿ On one level (albeit in a mountain setting).
🚌 Malaga or Granada Airport , coach to Granada then pickup by Cortijo Arunachala's own 4x4 vehicle.

Focus Advaita Vedanta (non-duality teaching open to all faiths)

Cortijo Romero

Janice Gray
22 Cottage Offices
Latimer Park
Latimer
Chesham
Buckinghamshire
HP5 1TU

© 01494 765775
℡ 01494 766577
✆ bookings@cortijo-romero.co.uk

✔ **Retreat House**
✔ **Holiday Operator**
✔ **Own Course Programme**
✔ **Venue for hire**
group full board (£25 to £50), large indoor space, several small spaces
⊸ 10 singles, 7 twins, 2 doubles and 2 apartments.
🍽 Exclusively vegetarian.
♿ Terraced site with limited wheelchair access.
🚌 Málaga then 2 hours by minibus.

Yearround alternative holidays in Spain.

Deep in the South of Spain, in a magnificent setting between the mountains and the sea, is Cortijo Romero, a jewelled oasis ...

A stunningly beautiful, unspoilt environment; mountains, rivers, ancient hill villages and the nearby fabled city of Granada. Delightful buildings in a typical Andalucian style, with beautiful gardens and orchards, set in an 800-year old olive grove. A superb pool surrounded by masses of flowers throughout the year, palm trees, and shaded courtyards. Comfortable rooms, all with bath or shower. Delicious food, with a wide variety of local produce.

A warm and supportive atmosphere, with a devoted and knowledgeable Anglo-Spanish staff.

The best climate in Europe, with 315 days of sunshine per year. Average temperatures are 7-10°C (15-18°F) above London, the humidity is low and the annual rainfall a mere 15in. Holiday Courses in Personal Development include Alexander Technique, Bodywork, Serious Fun, Creative Expression, Dance

and Music, Embodying the Spirit, Getting Out Of Your Own Way, Massage and Inspiration, Flamenco Dance, Living With Heart And Soul, The Challenge to Be Alive, T'ai Chi, Voice and Movement, Yoga and lots more ... Plus optional sessions of expressive dance, flamenco, structured counselling, massage, reflexology, shiatsu, Thai yoga ... Not to mention lazing by the pool, good company, excursions to ancient villages and wild countryside.

Development, Community, Celebration!

Subject Specialities
Body & breathwork, inner process, meditation, self expression, group process, ritual & shamanic, counselling, local culture, self-development, voice & dance.

Suitability or Specialism
Adults.

Cortijo Rosina

Location
Our home and farm occupy 40 acres of hilly land in the Alpujarras of southern Spain where we enjoy spectacular views of whitewashed villages and the Sierra Nevadas. We combine organic farming with creating a special place for individual and group retreats.

Programmes
Facilitated programmes and workshops: music, writing, mind body spirit, transformation, coaching, yoga, meditation, healing.
Individual time-out retreats with options: yoga, meditation, massage, reiki, coaching, walks, local tours.
What makes us different?
We offer a glimpse of a very different lifestyle. One where warmth, love and personal understanding are a way of life here in the Alpujarras. After 3.5 years of world travel, we discovered this unbelievable location to create and share the newest chapter of our lives.
We know that our visitors often come on retreat to think through issues/challenges or to plot a new course for the future. Our skills as personal coaches and facilitators are available to you. We welcome people looking for a peaceful and natural place to be. Non-smokers only.

Eco-tourism features
Natural spring water. Solar power. 40 acres of organic almonds, olives, figs, grapes and vegetables.

Michael & Rosie Sinclair
Cortijo Rosina
Los Almendrillos
Cadiar
Granada
ES-18440
Spain
℡ 00 34 958 343036
✎ cortijorosina@yahoo.co.uk

✔ **Retreat House**
✔ **Own Course Programme**
⌐ We have lovingly and creatively converted the stables and storage area into a self-contained apartment. It has a spacious main room with kitchen area and open fireplace. There's sufficient space for yoga, t'ai chi etc. One double, one single and a bathroom complete the accommodation.
♿ None.
🚗 Plane to Málaga or Almería then bus or pickup to Cadiar (3h or 1.5h respectively).
Focus Holistic

Garden of Light

http://www.thegardenoflight.net

Lourdes
Apdo correos 1126
Ibiza
ES-07800
Spain

℗ 00 34 71 33 46 44
✆ 00 34 71 33 46 44
✍
thegardenoflight@hotmail.com

✔ **Retreat House**
✔ **Bed & Breakfast**
✔ **Holiday Operator**
✔ **Own Course Programme**
✔ **Venue for hire**
group full board (from £33.50), large indoor space
⌁ 30 bedspaces.
🍽 Exclusively vegetarian.

Focus
New Age, Human growth

El Jardin de Luz. Situated between two worlds – Europe and Africa, rising out of the crystal clear waters of the Mediterranean Sea, lies the magic island of Ibiza. In the north of the island, secluded among indigenous forests and exotic gardens, The Garden of Light offers a beautiful and peaceful setting for residential seminars and workshops. The Centre features a group room which is light and well-equipped; large terraces for working in the open-air; capacity for 34 guests, pure drinking water from a natural spring; and serves delicious vegetarian meals with an oriental touch. The sunny and warm climate will enchant you, as will the beautiful sandy beaches, which can be found within walking distance of the Centre.

Suitability or Specialism
Adults.

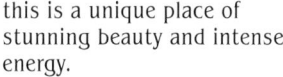
On the Canarian island La Gomera, following the stony road behind the harbour of Valle Gran Rey, you'll find our Finca Argayall. Situated in its own bay, embedded between the ocean and the mountains,

this is a unique place of stunning beauty and intense energy.

An international community of around 20 people is living and working together here and offers space for individuals as well as for groups to combine holiday and healing, relaxation and self-experience, celebration and ...

Event Types
Guided group retreats, business retreats, own course programme, regeneration programmes.

Subject Specialities
Health & healing, alternative lifestyles & technology, group process, inner process, body & breathwork, self expression, meditation, food & gardening, permaculture, dolphins and whales.

Suitability or Specialism
Adults.

Valle Gran Rey
La Gomera
ES-38870
Canary Islands

© 00 34 922 697008
℡ 00 34 922 805551
✆ info@argayall.com

✔ **Own Course Programme**
⌇ 29 bedspaces (2 singles, 13 doubles.)
🍴 Exclusively vegetarian.
🚌 Flight to Tenerife Sur, ferry to La Gomera, taxi or bus to Valle Gran Rey.

Focus holistic

Yuva

http://www.vegiventures.com

Nigel Walker, Castle Cottage
Castle Acre, King's Lynn
Norfolk PE32 2AJ

© 01760 755888
✆ yuva@vegiventures.com

✔ **Retreat House**
✔ **Bed & Breakfast**
✔ **Holiday Operator**
✔ **Venue for hire**
group full board, large indoor space
⤻ 24 bedspaces (5 singles, 5 twins, 3 doubles, 3 family rooms.)
◉ Exclusively vegetarian, special diets.

Eco Holiday Village: peaceful mountain location, secluded cove for swimming and snorkelling, great vegetarian/vegan food. Centre available for hire.
Yuva is a holiday/retreat centre in south-west Turkey, on 40 acres of protected forest, an area of outstanding natural beauty, in the mountains, right by the sea. Local farmers cultivate ancient terraces, growing grains, fruit and olives. This is the perfect place to relax and enjoy a healthy holiday. Yuva, which means 'homestead' in old Turkish,

is run by Atilla Sevilmis and his family, extending warm traditional Turkish hospitality. The main accommodation is in 4 buildings, constructed of natural materials. Each building has 2 spacious twin/double rooms, overlooking the bay. There are also 5 log cabins, suitable as single rooms. All rooms have electricity and ensuite shower and toilet. Some of the larger rooms can be comfortably used as triples. The food is delicious Turkish style vegetarian/vegan. Yuva is suitable for groups of up to 24 people. There is a purpose built group-work/yoga platform with breathtaking views. Yuva has excellent swimming from its rocky cove or take the local bus to the lagoon and beach at Ölüdeniz, about 25 minutes drive. Optional activities from Ölüdeniz include:

scuba diving, paragliding, boat trips, archaeological excursions… The recently mapped 'Lycian Way', a long distance route, passes near to Yuva, making it ideal for walking and outdoor holidays/courses of all types. For groups of 10 or more, phone or email for details and special low rates. For individual/family holidays ask for VegiVentures holiday brochure.

Event Types
Guided group retreats, self directed retreats, business retreats, working holidays.

Suitability or Specialism
Adults, couples, women, men, young people 12 to 17.

Eco-tourism features
Organic home-grown food, where possible. Buildings are of natural materials. Solar hot water heating. Deep respect for local traditions.

Other Places and Organisations

FRANCE

Agora Centre
Le Lac, Seignalens
FR-11240 France
Holiday Operator

Beau Champ
Montpeyroux, Dordogne
FR-24610 France
Community

Bellenau
Château Bel Enault
Saint-Côme-du-Mont
Carentan, Normandy
FR-50500 France
Venue for hire

Le Cerf Gris
4 Rue de la Paix, Moux
FR-11700 France
Own Course Programme

Ecolonie
1 Thietry
Hennezel, Vosges
FR-88260 France
Own Course Programme

Espace du Possible
8 Boulevard de Suzac
Meschers-sur-Gironde
FR-17132 France
Own Course Programme

Lavaldieu
Rennes-le-Château
FR-11190 France
Own Course Programme

La Maison Verte
31 Avenue Henri Mas
Roujan
FR-34320 France
Venue for hire

Les Peyrouses
Les Peyrouses
Bonnac
FR-09100 France
Own Course Programme

Le Plessis
Plumaudan
FR-22350 France
Venue for hire

Under the Lime Tree
Le Tilleul
Fontfaix le Haut
Cellefrouin
FR-16260 France
Own Course Programme

GERMANY

Predigerseminar Celle
Ev.-luth. Landeskirche
Hannovers, Berlinstr.4, Celle
DE-29223 Germany
Retreat House

GREECE

Galini Holidays
Box 6064, Koroni, Messinias
GR-24004 Greece
Holiday Operator

Other Places and Organisations

Peligoni Club
PO Box 88, Chichester
West Sussex PO20 7DP
Holiday Operator

Spirit of Life Centre
Henleaze Centre
13 Harbury Road, Henleaze
Bristol   BS9 4PN
Holiday Operator

**West Crete Holidays
and Holistic Centre**
The Old Olive Mill
Potamida 137, Kissamos, Crete
GR-73400 Greece
Holiday Operator

Yoga Plus
177 Ditchling Road, Brighton
East Sussex BN1 6JB
Holiday Operator

Yoga Practice
122 Lower Marsh
London SE1 7AE
Holiday Operator

Skyros Holistic Holidays
92 Prince of Wales Road
London NW5 3NE
Holiday Operator
also in
THAILAND

INDIA

Purple Valley Yoga Centre
c/o 4 Chapel Street
Penzance
Cornwall
TR18 4AJ
Retreat House

**Shanti Bhavan Yoga
and Massage Centre**
Silent Valley
Kovalam, Kerala
IN-695521
India
info@shantibhavanyoga
Own Course Programme

Yogamagic Canvas Hotel
care of 8 New Adel Avenue
Leeds
LS16 6BE
Holiday Operator

IRELAND

BrookLodge & Wells Spa
Macreddin Village
County Wicklow
Ireland
Health Spa

**Burren Yoga and
Meditation Centre**
Lig do Scith
Cappaghmore, Kinvara
County Galway
Ireland
Own Course Programme

**Cussens Cottage Vegan
Guest House**
Ballygrennan
Bulgaden, Kilmallock
County Limerick
Ireland
Bed & Breakfast

Green Lodge
Pearson's Bridge, Ballylickey
Bantry, County Cork
Ireland
Bed & Breakfast

The Healing Path
Ballytouhey, Clare Island
County Mayo
Ireland
Holiday Operator

Lios Dána Holistic Centre
Inch-Annascaul, County Kerry
Ireland
Retreat House

The Lodge and Spa
Inchydoney Island
Clonakilty, County Cork
Ireland
Health Spa

Rathe House
Kilmainham Wood, Co Meath
Ireland
Venue for hire

Shiplake Mountain Hostel
Dunmanway, County Cork
Ireland
Bed & Breakfast

Skyhil Camping
Skyhil
Glengarriff
Bantry, County Cork
Ireland
℡ 00353 27 63610
Camping

Sunyata Retreat Centre
Snata
Sixmilebridge
County Clare
Ireland
Retreat House

ITALY

Agoy
c/o 20 The Avenue
London
NW6 7YD
Holiday Operator

Art & Dolce Vita
Via Palica Tiburzi 32
San Polo Sabino (RI)
IT-02040
Italy
Own Course Programme

The Hill That Breathes
c/o Neals Yard Agency
BCM Neals Yard
London WC1N 3XX
Holiday Operator

In Sabina Yoga Centre
Via Pizzuti 53
Torri in Sabina
IT-02049
Italy
Venue for hire

Sunflower Retreat Holidays
Via Tito Tazo Nº 11
Casperia   CAP
IT-02041
Italy
℡ 0116 259 9422
✉ sunflowerretreats@ tiscalinet.it
🖥 www.sunflowerretreats.com
Holiday Operator

Other Places and Organisations

A Colina Atlântica
Quinta das Maçãs
Travessa dos Melquites 3
Barrantes, Salir de Matos
PT-2500-621 Portugal
Holiday Operator

El Bosque
C/ Del Guerrero 5
Mataelpino, Madrid
ES-28492 Spain
Own Course Programme

Eco Forest
Apdo 29
Coín
Málaga
ES-29100 Spain
Holiday Operator

Ibiza Yoga
8 Camden Road
London
NW1 9DP
Own Course Programme

Mas Collades
Carretera de Balsereny
a Avinyó Km 4
Balsareny
Catalunya
ES-08660
Spain
Venue for hire

Montaña Palmera
El Cañuelo
Periana
Málaga
ES-29710 Spain
✆ 0034 952 536506
✉ montpalmera@hotmail.com
🕸 www.montanapalmera.com
Own Course Programme

La Serrania
Apartment 211
Pollença
Mallorca
ES-07460
Spain
Retreat House

Taiyoga
Victoria Cottage
27 Darracott Road
Southbourne
Bournemouth
Dorset BH5 2AY
Holiday Operator

SRI LANKA

Barberyn Ayurveda Resorts
Barberyn Reef Hotel
Beruwala
Sri Lanka
Holiday Operator

Ulpotha
c/o Neal's Yard Agency
BCM Neal's Yard
London
WC1N 3XX
Holiday Operator

TURKEY

Health & Yoga Holidays
133a Devonshire Road
London
SE23 3LZ
✆ 020 8291 7981
Holiday Operator

Huzur Vadisi
c/o 12 Trinity Road
Aberystwyth
Ceredigion
SY23 1LU
Holiday Operator

Holiday and Tour Operators

PLACES TO BE

Nirvana Travel

Miss Rebecca Michaelides
Nirvana Travel
PO Box 10
Petra
Lesvos Island
GR-81109
Greece

© 00 30 22530 41991
✆ 00 30 22530 41992
✉ nirvanat@otenet.gr

✔ **Agent**
✔ **Holiday Operator**

Nirvana Travel was established in 1995 and operates in all fields of the travel industry in Greece, both incoming and out-going. Based in Petra on Lesvos Island, Greece's third largest island, with international and domestic airport services, Nirvana Travel's unique organization offers companies and individuals a personalised service from arrival right the way through to the point of departure. We can assist you with all sorts of activities that are linked with Main Stream Tourism – from boat trips to accommodation in main tourist areas – but also with Special Interest Breaks/Activities and requirements for individuals: from accommodation with character to bird watching, trekking, diving, cycling, painting, pottery, health breaks, Greek culture – food (cooking) and drink (tasting), Greek Language courses with traditional dancing – and many more health orientated activities such as Yoga, massage, reflexology and natural hot springs.

Come and enjoy the island's wonders and beauty with Rebecca, her friends and carefully selected associates.

Services Provided

Transfers, airline & ferry tickets, accommodation, car, bike & yacht hire, foreign exchange, bus & boat trips, conference & seminar organization, honeymoon & wedding organization and the holidays listed below.

Types of Holidays & Tour Packages Available

Cycling , Bird watching, Greek Cooking, Greek Language and Dance, Yoga, Horse Riding, Walking, Spa Health, Painting, Pottery, Watersports, Olive Picking, Pilgrimage, Jeep Safaris, Historical.
We cater for everyone: from individual to small personal groups and large groups.

Accommodation

We co-operate with people who run all types of units: from traditional studios, apartments and houses/villas to hotels of all categories.

Destinations

Lesvos Island. All of Greece: mainland and islands. Turkish coast and Istanbul.

Agent for holidays in Greece and Turkey

VegiVentures

VegiVentures provides holidays with great vegetarian/vegan food and "A touch of healthy living." Founded in 1989 by Swiss-trained chef and yoga teacher Nigel Walker, destinations now include holidays in Britain, Turkey and Peru. Some holidays are very laid back, eg Turkey, relax on the terrace enjoying the stunning sea and mountain views, stroll around ancient sites or chill-out on a secluded beach. The Lake District holidays invite you to breathe in lungfulls of fresh mountain air while stretching your legs over England's most beautiful hills and valleys. Peru is more challenging, thrilling high altitude journeys into the land of the Incas. Prices range from a "Creativity Weekend" in the UK for £79, Christmas houseparty on Exmoor from £199 for 4 nights, to 3 weeks in Peru for about £1250 (excluding flights). All holidays are ideal for men, women and couples. Phone or email for a free brochure.

Location
Europe including the UK, Middle East and North Africa, South America.

Types of Holiday
Small group, tailor made, working holidays, walking.

Subject Specialities
Local culture, ancient sites, arts & crafts, yoga, creativity, meditation.

Suitability or Specialism
Adults, couples, young people 12 to 17. People recovering from illness, average fitness levels.

Nigel Walker
Castle Cottage
Castle Acre
King's Lynn
Norfolk
PE32 2AJ

℡ 01760 755888
⌨ holidays@vegiventures.com

✔ **Holiday Operator**
✔ **Own Course Programme**

🍽 Exclusively vegetarian.

Wild and Free

PO Box 5872
Forres
Morayshire
IV36 1WA

© 0845 345 9052
✆ 0845 345 9052
✉ info@dolphinswims.co.uk

✔ **Holiday Operator**

Wild and Free offer a range of eco-friendly Dolphin Swims, Desert Safaris, Scuba Diving and Nature Holidays in beautiful locations around the world – as shown on BBC TV with Olympic gold medallist Sharron Davies.

Swim with wild dolphins
In the warm clear waters of the Red Sea a coral reef is home to a large group of Spinner Dolphins. This is a unique opportunity to be with dolphins in their natural environment. Other options include desert excursions by horse, camel or jeep.

Ecovillage accommodation. Full board, transfers and dolphin-swims are included.

Recent guest have said:
"We had an incredible time. We swam on our own with 60 or 70 dolphins for more than an hour. It was perfect bliss ..."

"We had the most fabulous holiday and we completed our mission of swimming with dolphins beyond what we could have ever imagined."

"My first day on the reef with the dolphins was a wicked experience, something I find that words do no justice to. I felt at peace with myself and all in the world, I felt humble compared with the magnificence of these awesome creatures and privileged to be among them in their own environment. I have already decided to return. I fell in love with the place, with the reef, the dolphins, the people and the fact that I felt I was at home."

Suitable for
Families, individuals and small groups.

Also available
Sinai Desert Bedouin Safaris, Dolphins and Whales around the world, Scuba Dive the Red Sea.

Eco-tourism features
We work in association with International Dolphin Watch (www.idw.org) and visit only dolphins and animals that are truly wild and free.

Yoga of the Heart

Heart Yoga is movement from the core of our being. Our body has the intelligence to know how it needs to move. The classical yoga postures or asanas developed from this intelligence. The structure developed for the asanas is known as Hatha Yoga.

Heart Yoga takes the classical asanas together with the philosophy and spiritual aspects of yoga and teaches them in a way that can transform the body, mind and emotions – touching the heart of our being.

We each have an innate ability to feel what is needed in our body, and each of us has unique needs. We come to understand ourselves and others through our own practice of asana, pranayama and meditation.

Heart Yoga is a growing school with teachers all over the UK. We also offer holidays, teachers awareness courses and have various books and videos to support your own learning and practice. Explore our website to find out more.

Louise Pagliaro
71 Rival Moor Road
Petersfield
Hampshire
GU31 4HX

✆ 01730 261001
✆ 01730 261001
✍
jenny@yoga-of-the-heart.org.uk

✔ **Retreat House**
✔ **Holiday Operator**
✔ **Own Course Programme**

Other Places and Organisations

Alternative Holidays UK
4 Alexandra Gardens
Ebury Road, Sherwood Rise
Nottingham NG5 1BA
Holiday Operator

**BAOBAB -
Alternative Roots to
Travel**
Old Fallings Hall
Old Fallings Lane
Wolverhampton WV10 8BL
Holiday Operator

Bicycle Beano
Erwood, Builth Wells
Powys LD2 3PQ
Holiday Operator

The Big Stretch
3 Florence Street
London N1 2DX
Holiday Operator

Buddhafield
c/o Trevince House
Hittisleigh, Exeter
Devon EX6 6LP
Camps

Community Action Treks
Warwick Mill
Warwick Bridge, Carlisle
Cumbria CA4 8RR
Holiday Operator

Dance Holiday Company
Carefree Travel Int Ltd
Zurich House
East Park, Crawley
West Sussex RH10 6AJ
Holiday Operator

Dolphin Connection
Second Floor
46 Osmond Road
Hove
East Sussex
BN3 1TD
Holiday Operator

Eco-resorts
1535 Chatham Colony Court
Reston
Virginia
VA-20190
United States of America
Holiday Operator

Encounter
Camp Green
Debenham
Stowmarket
Suffolk
IP14 6LA
Holiday Operator

**Erna Low Body & Soul
Holidays**
9 Reece Mews
London
SW7 3HE
Holiday Operator

Exodus
9 Weir Road
London
SW12 0LT
Holiday Operator

Footprint Adventures
5 Malham Drive
Lincoln
LN6 0XD
Holiday Operator

Free Spirit Travel
153 Carden Avenue, Brighton
East Sussex BN1 8LA
Alternative Travel Agent

Gorgeous Goddess
62 Falkner Street
Liverpool L8 7QA
Holiday Operator

Harmony Journeys
23 Severn Drive
Walton-on-Thames
Surrey
KT12 3BH
Holiday Operator

HF Holidays
Imperial House
Edgware Road
London NW9 5AL
Holiday Operator

High Places
Globe Centre
Penistone Road
Sheffield S6 3AE
Holiday Operator

in:spa retreats
35 Brompton Road
London SW3 1DE
Holiday Operator

In-Spirit Journeys
PO Box 26183
Hout Bay, Cape Town
ZA-7872 South Africa
Holiday Operator

Indus Tours
MWB Exchange
2 Gayton Road
Harrow, Middlesex
HA1 2XU
Holiday Operator

Kameleon Holidays
14 Landons Close
Prestons Road
London E14 9QQ
Holiday Operator

KE Adventure Travel
32 Lake Road, Keswick
Cumbria CA12 5DQ
Holiday Operator

Naturally Morocco
The Manse
Porthyrhyd
Carms
SA32 8PN
Holiday Operator

Naturetrek
Cheriton Mill
Alresford
Hampshire
SO24 0NG
Holiday Operator

Nepalese Trails
Random Cottage, Pentre
Llanfyllin, Powys SY22 5LE
Holiday Operator

Neals Yard Agency
BCM Neals Yard
London WC1N 3XX
℅ 0870 444 2702
✆ info@nealsyardagency.com
🖫 www.nealsyardagency.com
Agents for:
Barberyn p130
Cornish Tipi Holidays p87
Cortijo Romero p122
Health and Yoga Hols p130
The Hill that Breathes p129
Huzur Vadisi p130
Peligoni Club p128
Ulpotha p130

Palanquin Travels Ltd
Ray Powell Travel Ltd
42 High Street
Wanstead E11 2RJ
Holiday Operator

Other Holistic Holiday and Tour Operators

Other Places and Organisations

Pure Portugal
info@pureportugal.co.uk
www.pureportugal.co.uk
Alternative Travel Agents

Realworld Travel
Lower Farm
Happisburgh
Norwich NR12 0QQ
Alternative Travel Agents

Retreats Beyond Dover
St Etheldreda's Church
14 Ely Place
London EC1N 6RY
Holiday Operator

Sandra Straw Spiritual Holidays
112 Broadfield Estate
Broadhurst Gardens
London NW6 3QR
Holiday Operator

Sherpa Expeditions
131a Heston Road, Hounslow
Middlesex TW5 0RD
Holiday Operator

Spirit Visions
Wellsprings of Arnemetiae
Fern House
Ferd Road, Buxton
Derbyshire SK17 9NE
Holiday Operator

Tasting Places
Unit 108, Buspace Studios
Conlan Street
London W10 5AP
Own Course Programme

Walks Worldwide
Kings Arms Building
15 Main Street, High Bentham
Lancaster LA2 7LG
Holiday Operator

West London Yogashala
Basement, 22 Cleveland Trce
Bayswater
London W2 6QH
Holiday Operator

Wilderness Walks
35 Nursery Close, Whitstable
Kent CT5 1PD
Holiday Operator

Window to the World
44a Royar Thoppu, Srirangam
Trichy, Tamil Nadu
IN-620006 India
Holiday Operator

The Women's Retreat
106 Green Lane
St Albans
Hertfordshire
AL3 6EX
Holiday Operator

World Expeditions
4 Northfields Prospect
Putney Bridge Road
London
SW18 1PE
Holiday Operator

World Spirit
12 Vale Road
Altrincham
Cheshire
WA14 3AQ
Holiday Operator

Bed & Breakfast Seeker's Index

The B&B Seeker's Index is fairly self-explanatory. The entries listed have all said that they offer bed and breakfast and/or full board to individuals. However, standards may vary enormously and will range from conventional (and often) salubrious tourist board recommended venues to very unconventional intentional communities that offer a B&B option to visitors as one way of giving a short-term taste of their lifestyle. So please phone ahead, not only to check on availability but also to make sure that you know exactly what you're going to.

Vegetarian means that the establishment say they are exclusively vegetarian; some of these will be exclusively vegan (see their full page entry) – and of course they may well cater for more restrictive *Special Diets* within that basic parameter.

No smoking usually means within buildings – there may sometimes be a special smoking room.

Children over 5 and *Children under 5* refer to the suitability of the venue to children in those age ranges. A very few places have said that they can offer a *Children Minding* service but don't expect this to be available on demand.

Whlchr Access indicates a level of accessibility to wheelchair users. Some places give more details of access in their full page listing.

Max B&B shows the maximum daily charge for B&B where this has been stated – please make allowances for changes over time.

page number	Venue	Individ B&B	Individ full board	Veget-arian	No Smoking	Special Diets	Children over 5	Children under 5	Child Minding	Whlchr Access	Max B&B
East of England											
34	St Claret	◆	◆		◆		◆	◆			£35
Midlands											
38	The Grange	◆			◆	◆	◆	◆		◆	
43	Woodbrooke	◆	◆		◆	◆	◆				
Wales											
47	Anglesey Healing	◆				◆					
49	Coleg Trefeca	◆	◆		◆	◆	◆	◆		◆	
51	Heartspring	◆		◆	◆	◆	◆	◆			£42
52	Woodlands	◆			◆		◆				£29
58	Trigonos	◆			◆	◆		◆		◆	£28.50
South West England											
63	Ammerdown Centre	◆	◆		◆	◆	◆	◆		◆	
65	Beacon Centre	◆		◆	◆	◆	◆	◆			£18
66	Beech Hill	◆	◆		◆	◆	◆	◆		◆	£15
67	Boswednack Manor	◆		◆	◆	◆		◆			£24
72	Hawkwood	◆	◆		◆	◆				◆	
73	Hazelwood House	◆	◆			◆	◆	◆		◆	£37
74	Leela Centre	◆	◆	◆	◆	◆	◆	◆		◆	£17.50
75	Little Burrows	◆	◆	◆	◆	◆	◆	◆		◆	£29
76	Lower Shaw	◆	◆	◆	◆	◆	◆	◆	◆	◆	£15

page number	Venue	Individ B&B	Individ full board	Veget-arian	No Smoking	Special Diets	Children over 5	Children under 5	Child Minding	Whlchr Access	Max B&B
77	Michael House	♦		♦	♦	♦	♦				£29.50
78	Middle Piccadilly	♦	♦	♦	♦						£30
79	Monkton Wyld	♦	♦	♦	♦	♦	♦	♦			£37
81	St Peter's Grange	♦	♦		♦	♦	♦	♦		♦	£25
82	Samways	♦		♦		♦					
83	Self Realization	♦	♦		♦	♦					
84	Shekinashram	♦		♦	♦	♦					£27
85	Tordown	♦		♦	♦		♦	♦			£35
86	Wild Pear	♦				♦					£18
South East England											
92	The Abbey	♦	♦	♦	♦	♦					£30
93	Braziers	♦	♦		♦	♦	♦				£26
97	Douai Abbey	♦	♦		♦	♦	♦	♦			£33
98	Park Place	♦	♦		♦					♦	£26
Outside the UK											
107	Le Blé en Herbe	♦	♦	♦	♦	♦	♦				
111	Gaia Visions	♦		♦	♦						
112	White Mountain	♦	♦		♦	♦	♦				
113	Beach and Lake	♦				♦					
119	Phoenix	♦	♦	♦	♦	♦	♦	♦		♦	
126	Yuva	♦	♦	♦	♦	♦	♦				

Bed & Breakfast Seeker's Index

Retreat Seeker's Index

This is the index for you if you're looking for a retreat. Of primary concern to you will probably be whether the venue adheres to a particular faith or has a specific spiritual orientation. For this reason the different places appear in the index grouped according to their spiritual focus. First there are the places that have no particular orientation or else have a focus with few representatives in the book. Eco-spiritual and New Age are popular modern orientations. Christian and Buddhist retreat houses respectively are grouped together but you may find more specific classifications on the venue's own page. **Group** means that they offer guided retreats for groups; **Individ** means guided retreats for individuals; **Self D** generally means that a supportive environment is provided for people who are directing their own retreats. **Business** means that a retreat environment can be offered to groups from commercial and voluntary organisations. **Progs** refers to the availability of programmes for healing and recovery to assist people who are coming out of some kind of crisis. **Medit** and **Prayer** means that instruction in meditation and prayer are amongst the specialities on offer. **Whlchr** indicates a level of wheelchair access; some organisations give more details in their full page entry.

page	Venue	Region	Group	Individ	Self D	Business	Progs	Medit	Prayer	Whlchr
20	Brightlife	North of England	◆			◆		◆		
21	Eastgate	North of England	◆	◆	◆	◆	◆	◆		
26	Orange Tree	North of England	◆	◆	◆	◆	◆	◆		◆
39	Holycombe	The Midlands			◆		◆			
41	Time Away	The Midlands			◆		◆			
50	Fort Belan	Wales			◆	◆		◆		
51	Heartspring	Wales		◆	◆		◆	◆		
52	Woodlands	Wales			◆			◆		
53	Life Foundation	Wales	◆					◆		

page	Venue	Region	Group	Individ	Self D	Business	Progs	Medit	Prayer	Whlchr
55	Old Rectory	Wales			◆	◆		◆		
56	Pen Rhiw	Wales	◆					◆		◆
57	Spirit Horse	Wales	◆				◆	◆	◆	
58	Trigonos	Wales			◆			◆		◆
72	Hawkwood	South West England	◆		◆	◆		◆	◆	◆
73	Hazelwood House	South West England	◆		◆	◆				◆
75	Little Burrows	South West England	◆	◆	◆			◆		◆
78	Middle Piccadilly	South West England		◆	◆	◆				
80	Roseven	South West England	◆					◆	◆	
83	Self Realization	South West England	◆	◆	◆	◆	◆	◆	◆	
85	Tordown	South West England	◆	◆	◆					
86	Wild Pear	South West England	◆		◆			◆		
92	The Abbey	South East England	◆		◆	◆		◆		
93	Braziers	South East England	◆	◆	◆	◆		◆		
96	Commonwork	South East England			◆	◆				◆
100	Woodrow	South East England			◆					◆
108	La Buissière	Outside the UK								
110	Sun Centre	Outside the UK	◆		◆		◆	◆		
113	Beach and Lake	Outside the UK					◆			
116	Cloona	Outside the UK		◆			◆			

page	Venue	Region	Group	Individ	Self D	Business	Progs	Medit	Prayer	Whlchr
121	Cortijo Arunachala	Outside the UK	◆	◆	◆			◆		
122	Cortijo Romero	Outside the UK	◆	◆		◆	◆	◆		
126	Yuva	Outside the UK	◆		◆	◆				
135	Yoga of the Heart	UK and Elsewhere	◆							
Eco-Spiritual										
65	Beacon Centre	South West England	◆	◆			◆	◆		
68	EarthSpirit	South West England	◆				◆	◆		◆
84	Shekinashram	South West England	◆		◆			◆		
111	Gaia Visions	Outside the UK	◆	◆		◆		◆		
112	White Mountain	Outside the UK			◆			◆		
114	Friday's Place	Outside the UK			◆					
Christian										
23	Lattendales	North of England			◆		◆	◆	◆	◆
24	Loyola Hall	North of England	◆	◆				◆	◆	◆
27	Rookhow Centre	North of England	◆		◆	◆		◆		
28	St Oswald's	North of England	◆	◆	◆				◆	◆
33	All Hallows	East of England		◆						
34	St Claret	East of England	◆	◆	◆	◆	◆			
63	Ammerdown Centre	South West England	◆	◆	◆			◆	◆	◆
81	St Peter's Grange	South West England	◆	◆	◆				◆	◆

page	Venue	Region	Group	Individ	Self D	Business	Progs	Medit	Prayer	Whlchr
94	Charney Manor	South East England	◆		◆	◆		◆	◆	◆
95	Claridge House	South East England	◆	◆	◆		◆	◆		
97	Douai Abbey	South East England	◆	◆	◆	◆		◆	◆	
98	Park Place	South East England	◆	◆	◆			◆		◆
99	Seekers Trust	South East England			◆			◆	◆	
115	Chrysalis	Outside the UK			◆		◆	◆		
	Buddhist									
14	Shanti Griha	Scotland	◆	◆	◆			◆		
25	Manjushri	North of England	◆					◆		
64	The Barn	South West England	◆			◆	◆	◆		
67	Boswednack Manor	South West England	◆	◆			◆	◆		
70	Gaia House	South West England	◆	◆	◆			◆		
	New Age									
13	Newbold	Scotland			◆					
47	Anglesey Healing	Wales	◆		◆			◆		
54	Neuadd-Isaf	Wales			◆					
106	Sanctuary	Outside the UK	◆	◆		◆		◆	◆	
117	Dunderry Park	Outside the UK	◆		◆	◆	◆	◆		
123	Cortijo Rosina	Outside the UK	◆	◆	◆	◆	◆	◆		
124	Garden of Light	Outside the UK	◆	◆	◆		◆	◆	◆	

Workshop Seeker's Index

The types of places listed in this book are (quite rightly) very resistant to classification. However, for the book to be useful a degree of classification is necessary. The categories are meant to be starting points. Venues will describe what they offer in more detail in their written descriptions. The S-codes in this index are explained in the list alongside. Places will offer courses and workshops within these broad subject areas but not necessarily everything that is described.

S1 Arts & Crafts
drawing; painting; pottery; etc
S2 Self expression
music; writing; drama, etc
S3 Bodywork & Breathwork
yoga; t'ai chi; massage; bio-energetics; breathwork; rebirthing; etc
S4 Health & Healing
acupressure; aromatherapy; homeopathy; psychic healing; etc
S5 Outdoor activities & Sport
walking; climbing; inner sport; etc
S6 Conservation work
woodland work; hedge laying; etc
S7 Food & Gardening
diet modification; cookery; organic gardening; permaculture;
S8 Alternative lifestyles & technology
communal living; technology; etc
S9 Counselling
spiritual; psychotherapeutic; individuals; couples; etc
S10 Inner process
dreamwork; gestalt; hypnosis; regression; etc
S11 Group process
teamwork; trust building; psychodrama; etc
S12 Ritual & Shamanic
vision quest; ancient wisdom; ceremony; etc
S13 Earth mysteries
ancient sites; geomancy; etc
S14 Meditation
guided visualisation; attunement; inner listening; concentration; etc
S15 Prayer
contemplative; devotional; chanting; mantras; etc

work means that they can sometimes offer working holidays to people.

acc means that some of the courses on offer carry accreditation.

teach means that they run teacher training courses.

page	Venue	S1	S2	S3	S4	S5	S6	S7	S8	S9	S10	S11	S12	S13	S14	S15	work	acc	teach
	Scotland																		
12	Findhorn	♦	♦		♦		♦	♦	♦		♦	♦			♦	♦		♦	
13	Newbold								♦						♦				
14	Shanti Griha	♦	♦	♦	♦	♦		♦	♦		♦				♦				♦
	North of England																		
20	Brightlife		♦	♦	♦						♦		♦	♦	♦				
21	Eastgate	♦	♦	♦	♦	♦					♦	♦			♦				
23	Lattendales				♦						♦				♦	♦			
25	Manjushri										♦				♦		♦		
26	Orange Tree			♦	♦	♦					♦				♦				
28	St Oswald's															♦			
	Midlands																		
38	The Grange	♦	♦	♦		♦					♦				♦	♦			
39	Holycombe		♦	♦	♦				♦				♦	♦					
43	Woodbrooke	♦	♦		♦			♦			♦			♦	♦	♦		♦	
	Wales																		
47	Anglesey Healing				♦	♦					♦			♦	♦				

page	Venue	S1	S2	S3	S4	S5	S6	S7	S8	S9	S10	S11	S12	S13	S14	S15	work	acc	teach
49	Coleg Trefeca	♦	♦													♦			
53	Life Foundation			♦	♦					♦					♦		♦		♦
56	Pen Rhiw										♦				♦				
57	Spirit Horse	♦	♦	♦	♦		♦		♦	♦	♦	♦	♦	♦	♦	♦	♦		
58	Trigonos	♦		♦	♦		♦	♦	♦		♦				♦				
	South West England																		
64	The Barn							♦	♦		♦	♦			♦		♦		
65	Beacon Centre	♦	♦	♦	♦			♦	♦	♦	♦	♦	♦		♦				
67	Boswednack Manor			♦										♦	♦				
70	Gaia House														♦				
71	Grimstone		♦	♦	♦		♦	♦	♦	♦	♦	♦	♦		♦		♦	♦	
72	Hawkwood	♦	♦	♦	♦				♦		♦	♦	♦	♦	♦	♦			
73	Hazelwood House			♦			♦	♦	♦					♦					
75	Little Burrows	♦	♦	♦	♦			♦	♦	♦	♦				♦				
76	Lower Shaw	♦	♦					♦	♦								♦		
78	Middle Piccadilly				♦														
79	Monkton Wyld	♦		♦	♦		♦		♦		♦	♦	♦		♦		♦	♦	

page	Venue	S1	S2	S3	S4	S5	S6	S7	S8	S9	S10	S11	S12	S13	S14	S15	work	acc	teach
113	Beach and Lake			♦	♦														
114	Friday's Place			♦	♦				♦										
115	Chrysalis			♦						♦	♦	♦			♦				
116	Cloona				♦														
117	Dunderry Park		♦	♦	♦	♦	♦	♦	♦	♦		♦	♦	♦	♦		♦	♦	♦
118	Ealaín Uisce	♦	♦		♦						♦		♦		♦		♦		
119	Phoenix		♦	♦	♦	♦	♦	♦	♦		♦				♦				
120	Moinhos Velhos				♦														
121	Cortijo Arunachala			♦							♦				♦				
122	Cortijo Romero		♦	♦						♦	♦	♦	♦		♦				
123	Cortijo Rosina		♦	♦	♦				♦	♦		♦			♦				
124	Garden of Light	♦	♦	♦	♦	♦		♦		♦	♦	♦		♦	♦	♦			♦
125	Argayall		♦	♦	♦			♦	♦		♦	♦			♦				
133	VegiVentures																		
135	Yoga of the Heart																	♦	♦

The Travel Agent for Inner Journeys

Reach your target audience

"Neal's Yard Agency is right on top with enquiry & booking responses, even better than *The Guardian*."

Huzur Vadisi, Alternative Holidays in Turkey

Let us inform the public & media about your retreats & holistic holidays

★**Spread the word:** reach more than 13,000, including 7,500 on our constantly updated mailing list. Be included in the quarterly *Holiday & Events Guide*, prices from only £24, or include a leaflet in our mailing.

★**Reach new facilitators to hire your venue** – 1050 up-to-date targeted contacts.

★**Neal's Yard Holiday Promotions Club** – reaching the imaginative explorer. Press releases, proactive outreach to the media, free & discounted entries in Guide and more.

To find out more
contact Ulrike or Corinne on Tel/Fax 0870 444 2702 or info@nealsyardagency.com
BCM Neal's Yard, London WC1N 3XX, UK, www.nealsyardagency.com

---

Neals Yard Agency

Venue Seeker's Index

The Venue Seeker's Index should be your first stop if you are a course facilitator or organiser looking for a place to run a workshop.

Venues are listed in ascending order of number of bedspaces (**beds**). Numbers of single, twin, double, family rooms and dormitories are shown in entries in the regional section.

Group B&B, **Group FB**, **Group SC**, refer to bed & breakfast, full board and self catering for groups. **Camp** means that camping is a possibility.

Large Space usually means that there is at least one large space available to the group and **Small Spaces** that several smaller spaces may be on offer.

Whlchr Access: some venues give more access details on their page. **No Smok** and **Special Diets** are fairly self explanatory.

There are as many charging systems as there are venues and inevitably prices change over time. Some price details are printed. Where a venue has quoted prices they are the full board charge per head for a 24 hour period. Some have given a minimum figure (**min 24h**), some a maximum (**max 24h**) and some none at all.

The search facility on the Places to Be website is particularly useful if you're looking for a venue in which to run a course, workshop or small conference.

Just select your region from a pop-up menu, key in the number of bedspaces that you're looking for, hit the "Search" button ... and a number of possibilities should appear. Click on them in turn in order to read about them, see a picture and, in most cases, link to a location map.

Page	Venue	location	beds	Group B&B	Group FB	Group SC	Camp	No Smok	Spec Diets	Whlchr Access	Large Space	Small Spaces	min 24h	max 24h
up to 10 bedspaces														
21	Eastgate	N Eng	6		◆	◆		◆	◆		◆			
114	Friday's Place	India	6		◆	◆			◆					
77	Michael House	SW Eng	6					◆	◆					
41	Time Away	Midlands	6		◆			◆	◆					£35
54	Neuadd-Isaf	Wales	7			◆						◆		
118	Ealaín Uisce	Ireland	8		◆			◆						€65
64	The Barn	SW Eng	9					◆	◆		◆	◆	£11	£17
78	Middle Piccadilly	SW Eng	9					◆			◆		£60	£80
67	Boswednack Manor	SW Eng	10	◆	◆			◆	◆		◆		£30	£50
20	Brightlife	N Eng	10						◆					
108	La Buissière	France	10			◆		◆						
75	Little Burrows	SW Eng	10	◆	◆	◆		◆	◆	◆	◆	◆	£40	£46
14	Shanti Griha	Scotland	10		◆			◆	◆		◆		£35	£35
11 to 20 bedspaces														
106	Sanctuary	Barbados	11		◆	◆					◆			
99	Seekers Trust	SE Eng	11											
110	Sun Centre	France	14		◆	◆		◆			◆	◆	£35	£38

Venue Seeker's Index

Page	Venue	location	beds	Group B&B	Group FB	Group SC	Camp	No Smok	Spec Diets	Whlchr Access	Large Space	Small Spaces	min 24h	max 24h
66	Beech Hill	SW Eng	15	◆	◆	◆	◆	◆	◆	◆	◆			£32
113	Beach and Lake	India	16		◆				◆					
28	St Oswald's	N Eng	16		◆			◆	◆	◆	◆	◆		
82	Samways	SW Eng	16		◆	◆			◆		◆	◆		
107	Le Blé en Herbe	France	17	◆	◆		◆	◆	◆		◆	◆		
69	East Down	SW Eng	17	◆	◆	◆			◆		◆			
26	Orange Tree	N Eng	17		◆			◆	◆	◆	◆		£75	£100
92	The Abbey	SE Eng	18	◆	◆	◆		◆	◆		◆	◆	£35	£50
39	Holycombe	Midlands	18		◆			◆			◆	◆		
115	Chrysalis	Ireland	20		◆	◆		◆	◆			◆		
55	Old Rectory	Wales	20			◆		◆			◆	◆		
27	Rookhow Centre	N Eng	20			◆	◆	◆			◆	◆		
112	White Mountain	Greece	20	◆	◆	◆	◆	◆	◆		◆	◆	£35	£60
21 to 30 bedspaces														
23	Lattendales	N Eng	21		◆	◆		◆	◆	◆	◆		£43	£43
80	Roseven	SW Eng	23			◆					◆			
65	Beacon Centre	SW Eng	24	◆	◆	◆	◆	◆	◆		◆	◆	£35	£35
122	Cortijo Romero	Spain	24		◆			◆			◆	◆	£25	£50

Page	Venue	location	beds	Group B&B	Group FB	Group SC	Camp	No Smok	Spec Diets	Whlchr Access	Large Space	Small Spaces	min 24h	max 24h
38	The Grange	Midlands	24	◆	◆			◆	◆	◆	◆	◆	£44	£54
126	Yuva	Turkey	24		◆			◆	◆		◆			
58	Trigonos	Wales	25	◆	◆			◆	◆	◆	◆	◆	£27	£45
86	Wild Pear	SW Eng	25	◆	◆	◆			◆		◆	◆	£30	£35
93	Braziers	SE Eng	28	◆	◆	◆	◆	◆	◆		◆	◆	£56	
124	Garden of Light	Spain	30		◆		◆	◆	◆		◆		£33.50	
76	Lower Shaw	SW Eng	30	◆	◆		◆	◆	◆	◆		◆	£30	£30
31 to 40 bedspaces														
117	Dunderry Park	Ireland	32		◆		◆	◆	◆		◆	◆	€65	€65
81	St Peter's Grange	SW Eng	33	◆	◆			◆	◆	◆	◆	◆	£35	£37
68	EarthSpirit	SW Eng	35	◆	◆		◆	◆	◆	◆	◆			
79	Monkton Wyld	SW Eng	35	◆	◆		◆	◆	◆		◆	◆	£37	£42
56	Pen Rhiw	Wales	35	◆	◆	◆		◆	◆		◆	◆	£43	£43
40	Poulstone Court	Midlands	36		◆			◆	◆		◆			
42	Unstone	Midlands	36	◆	◆	◆	◆		◆		◆	◆		
11	Burgh Lodge	Scotland	37		◆					◆	◆			
49	Coleg Trefeca	Wales	38	◆	◆			◆	◆	◆	◆	◆		
50	Fort Belan	Wales	40			◆		◆			◆	◆		

Venue Seeker's Index

Page	Venue	location	beds	Group B&B	Group FB	Group SC	Camp	No Smok	Spec Diets	Whlchr Access	Large Space	Small Spaces	min 24h	max 24h
71	Grimstone	SW Eng	40		◆			◆	◆	◆	◆	◆	£44	£48
34	St Claret	E Eng	40	◆	◆	◆		◆						
41 to 60 bedspaces														
94	Charney Manor	SE Eng	42		◆	◆		◆	◆	◆	◆	◆	£61.30	£67.50
96	Commonwork	SE Eng	45	◆	◆	◆	◆	◆	◆	◆	◆	◆	£76.38	£144.53
97	Douai Abbey	SE Eng	46	◆	◆	◆		◆	◆		◆	◆	£35	£43
72	Hawkwood	SW Eng	51		◆			◆	◆	◆	◆	◆		
100	Woodrow	SE Eng	53		◆		◆	◆	◆	◆	◆	◆		
22	Hebden House	N Eng	58	◆	◆			◆	◆	◆	◆	◆	£39.50	£47
73	Hazelwood House	SW Eng	60	◆	◆	◆	◆			◆	◆		£40	£70
98	Park Place	SE Eng	60	◆	◆	◆		◆		◆	◆	◆		
61+ bedspaces														
48	Buckland Hall	Wales	68		◆	◆		◆	◆	◆	◆	◆	£46	£68
63	Ammerdown Centre	SW Eng	70	◆	◆			◆	◆	◆	◆	◆	£36	£70
43	Woodbrooke	Midlands	70	◆	◆			◆	◆		◆	◆		
74	Leela Centre	SW Eng	72	◆	◆		◆	◆	◆	◆	◆	◆	£33	£50
33	All Hallows	E Eng	120		◆			◆	◆		◆	◆	£28.50	£42.50
57	Spirit Horse	Wales	200		◆	◆	◆	◆	◆		◆		£20	

Alphabetical Index

Do you run or do you know of a venue not listed in this edition of Places to Be?
Venues can join the listing on the web site — www.places-to-be.com — almost
instantly and then be eligible for inclusion in later printed editions of the book.
Fill out this postcard and return it to us. Don't forget the stamp.

Name of venue

Address

Postcode

Telephone number

Fax number

Electronic Mail and/or web site URL

Contact Name

How did you hear about Places to Be?

Dear Reader, We hope that you have found this edition of Places to Be to be both useful and
enjoyable. We welcome your feedback and invite you to fill out this postcard and return it to us.

Please tick one or both

☐ I run/organise workshops/courses ☐ I participate in workshops/courses

What are you looking for from a directory like this? Please score (1 = first)

☐ individual retreats ☐ group retreats ☐ venues to hire

☐ led workshops ☐ "alternative" B&Bs ☐ working holidays

☐ "alternative" holidays ☐ "alternative" tours ☐ ....

☐ Have you accessed the associated web site at www.places-to-be.com?

If yes, do you access the Internet

☐ at home? ☐ at work? ☐ elsewhere, eg library?

What features would you add to a future edition?

How did you hear about Places to Be?

Name

Address

Postcode

2005

Coherent Visions
BCM Visions
London
WCIN 3XX

Coherent Visions
BCM Visions
London
WCIN 3XX

2005

Coherent Visions
BCM Visions
London
WCIN 3XX